L H F   M D

Love, Humor, Faith: My Destiny

The Making of a Modern Medical Woman

LHF MD

Love, Humor, Faith: My Destiny

The Making of a Modern Medical Woman

BY L. H. FUGE, MD

Word Association Publishers
www.wordassociation.com

Printed in the United States of America

ISBN: 978-1-59571-262-2
Library of Congress Control Number: 2008923510

Word Association Publishers
205 Fifth Avenue
Tarentum, Pennsylvania 15084
www.wordassociation.com

TABLE OF CONTENTS

FAMILY OF MY FUTURE:

*Photos taken by LHF, MD personally

I dedicate this book to my children.
We taught each other that anything is possible
with Love, Determination and Prayer.

PREFACE
In My Daughter's Eyes

Still small since first glimpse, My Daughter changed my life. From my picking her special name: "Sikira," to choosing the mantra for her tenth birthday: "Aspire," she has been unique.

Prayers, Hopes, exams, medicines and surgeries marked our rocky lives' landscape. In those initial years, we celebrated each birthday with lavish abandon, not sure if Faith or Fate would bring another.

December 2003, public school, 4th grade Christmas show, Sikira sang the solo. Dramatic for the fact that since before she started school, My Daughter had no vision left.

Her eyes don't see our land, pond, pastures . . . forty acres: Promises Kept Farm. It's said land is marked by the flow of water and time. Our Landmarks are of tears and milestones of fulfilled promises. Last year, Sikira ran alone from our pond up the hill through our pasture. The steep grade her guide, wind in her face, ponytail flying, laughing, she left her younger brother breathless behind her.

My work shows My Daughter's impact. That day's photo graced our wall for months. Hope, Faith, frustrations, perseverance, good people, hard times and Love have built my angel. I am so proud of Sikira. Tears from her eyes, their depth when she ponders, their joy when she laughs, drive me to be more.

Well educated, a professional, yet it was seeing her strive that lead me to try after more than ten years to leave where I worked and form: "The Care Team," combining offices and caretakers in one place. Sikira's pictures are seen in nearly every room. Viewing them provides: entertainment, solace, guidance, or a beacon to patients, staff and me. **Sikira** is Our Blessing. My Daughter.

In My Daughter's eyes, I may seem better than I am; but because of her, I am better than I would have been.

(December 25, 2003 Inspired by Martina McBride's song of the same name)

Sikira with her ever-present tape player*

INTRODUCTION

This book is about remembrances, maybe a little romance, and certainly redemption. I share examples of how I have been taught and tested and blessed.

This is not a book of scandal or gossip or innuendo, containing the secrets and confidences of my patients. Not even my closest family learns such things. My husband never knows the people who are my patients unless they tell him so—even if they are family or friends. The topic of my medical clinical work is never allowed to come up at home. My children are often out with me in public when patients, their families, colleagues, or fellow health care workers, come up to me and start expounding on something private. As they share their personal, intimate concerns, they seem to be thinking of the children more as furniture, than the little tape recorders they actually are. By the age of three, my children had learned the word "confidential." They could say it clearly and knew that it meant, "It's a secret." Even when they were little, if someone would come up and start speaking to "Dr. Fuge," instead of Mommy, they would say knowingly and loudly, "That's confidential!" Many was the time that remark stopped people in mid-sentence.

I've had the honor and privilege of sharing in the lives of thousands over two and a half decades. I've gotten to deliver babies into this world, some of them to adolescent mothers on a rocky start, others to couples desperately grateful finally to have conceived after extended struggles. I delivered a child that the family knew had already died in the womb, baptized him, and laid him into their arms for farewell. I delivered another angel into their parents' arms before taking their photographs while they were married in our hospital that same day. Some of these youngsters I delivered, I've cared for through their young lives until they are starting to have their own children.

In my first eleven months in local private practice, I found seventy-three new, "primary" cancers. This was an awful burden of responsibility to find, inform and help these individuals and their families through their difficult ordeals. I've helped prevent many more. I've successfully resuscitated people when they've stopped breathing or their hearts have stopped. I've consoled the families of those who did not survive. I've counseled those despairing, abused or grieving. I've been privileged to hear life stories of many accomplished individuals in the community. I've known the joy of caring for three or four generations of the same families.

I've sacrificed of myself to become good at medicine and immersed myself in patient care. My calling has been to shoulder the awesome responsibility of not vacationing—or even sleeping at times—to help those in need through their moments of crisis. A physician, a person, can be a therapeutic tool herself, if she lets her spirit and her knowledge be available to others. That's what I've tried to do. I would not have been able to do what I have done in Medicine if it were not for my family and upbringing.

Family stories and my life experiences are retold here, just as I remember them or as they were recounted to me. When I share personal and private information, I do so in the hope that it will illuminate another's path through difficult times. I have tried to find a life lesson in each difficulty and something to be thankful for each day. In medicine, as in life, it has served me best to pay more attention to my disposition, than my circumstances. I try to "*Be* happy" rather than "*Be* a doctor". With God's help and family and friends' guidance and understanding, I hope to accomplish *both*. I pray that each of you find a path that brings you as much peace, joy and fulfillment.

I grew up loved and smiling. Dad modeled using Humor as a positive outlet, even in dire situations. He would quote: "Well outside of *that*, Mrs. Lincoln—how did you like the play?" His mother may have found him to be irreverent at times, but Grandma Nancy personified living with trust in God. Because of my "foundation" family, the elements of Love, Humor, and Faith are entwined in my destiny. I strive through my actions to make them part of my legacy.

I thank each person who's given me the opportunity to share with her or him. I share my story here for those who've known me a little and maybe wanted to know me better, for those who wondered and didn't ask, for those who are searching, hoping to find their own path in life. I write to acknowledge those who made it possible for me to do whatever I have done in this life.

God bless.
La Donna

The Fuges

CHAPTER ONE
My Destiny

My path was set in motion over Christmas as a child. I spent the day vomiting. My family finally, reluctantly, made the trip to the regional Children's Hospital in Pittsburgh, Pennsylvania.

"Virus," I think they said. I think that must be Latin for, "We have no idea." They, too, had difficulty managing this malady; I stayed in the hospital.

I recall isolation, being kept apart. I was all but tied to the bed, trussed up with IVs, to replace the body fluids I had been losing. For any parents to look at their child through a glass window would be difficult. For me, a child raised by two blind parents, not having my parents with me constantly was torture. In our family, there was no communication without touch. It was devastating.

When that ordeal was over, my family helped me to get over the emotional trauma of events by role-playing with my baby dolls. We hooked up their little IV by clothes pins. After that "therapy," I began attaching myself to the idea of filling the "gap that obviously existed" in hospitals for "good family doctors."

My parents were very private about vocalizing, let alone showing their affections. My sister, Kid and I recall them leaving the kitchen table to go to the hallway away from us to kiss goodbye. Hugs and kisses were for private moments.

Dad was especially frugal in showing his emotions. Neither pride nor affection were outwardly displayed. They just had to be understood. If I count in my adult life the number of times my father told me he was proud of me, I would still have fingers left on my hand. He would say, "I love you" as sparingly. For an eloquent speaker, he left a lot unspoken.

Dad was an attorney with a private law office. His private law library dated back to the 1800s. We were happy enough during the time I worked there with him, but it was not for me. Too much isolation. Not enough people contact. Despite my obvious interest in healthcare that started after my own hospital stay, I am not sure when my father actually wrapped his mind around the fact that I would not continue in that law office with him, nor in his profession.

Before I graduated from medical school, my father went out to our driveway where early life lessons had been taught. My own first car was tiny by comparison to Mom's 1975 Lincoln Towne Car. Dad affixed a personalized license plate to my vehicle: "LHF MD."

Although my dad did not use the words, "I'm proud of you," I am not sure which one of us was prouder in that moment, when he attached that prophetic set of five letters that would follow me from vehicle to vehicle, decade to decade.

It is funny that in Pennsylvania, a license plate only goes on the back of a vehicle. That one may have been more appropriate in the front, as those letters led me.

LaDonna H. Fuge as an infant

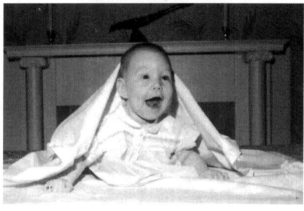

CHAPTER TWO
Precious Beginning

I was not a brilliant child but I'm told that Grandma Nancy had been known to say so. Perhaps like any other proud grandparent, it was wishful thinking or the result of superstition. She was known to comment that I had no hair to speak of for practically two years, just a tiny little wisp. She saw this as a sure sign of intelligence, just like her boy, the attorney, the other L.H. Fuge.

My father and I certainly share similar characteristics. Many of these would serve me in life, patience not necessarily being one of them.

Our folks' special day was the thirteenth. They met that date, married that date, and the obstetrician calculated that their first child would be born on April 13. The thirteenth was always a positive number in our world. But, impatient, I did not wait until the thirteenth. As often happens with children, time for delivery does not necessarily fit with their parents' plans. I was born on April 11.

Intelligent, well-spoken people themselves, my parents made sure I had my father's initials. I was the firstborn.

Mom desperately wanted a girl and was blessed with one. They chose a unique name from the French language they had both studied at Pittsburgh's School for the Blind, and my mother's French heritage. It came from the verb "to give." I was the gift they wanted. Mom's name, Dorothy means "the gift of God." In French, the word "the" before nouns is written as "Le" for masculine, "La" for feminine. I became "LaDonna", "The Gift."

For this gift, my mother retired from work and stayed home and began my education, long before I could do more than listen. I am the proud product of that very early education. My young, proud parents lavished attention and continuous instruction on me from the beginning. By age two, I had a vocabulary that even today, I would be hard pressed to spell correctly. I was tutored in the understanding of terms such as "project," "enunciate," and "articulate." I don't know if baby talk was ever used by others to me, but not by my parents. They taught counting first by handing me clothes pins. For dinner games, my Dad would have me do math problems out loud. We never used paper and pencil. I suppose it stimulated my thinking more. We used 3-D magnets on the refrigerator so I could learn the shapes of numbers and the alphabet.

I was teased later in life about being a walking, talking, seeing-eye dog. In part, it has to do with stories of my going to town as soon as I could walk with my mother. I proudly spelled out the name, size and prices on each item, on one shelf after another, in each store. The patience she must have had to put up with that plodding process of information gathering I can't imagine, let alone reproduce. She was a proud woman, perhaps sometimes too proud to want to ask an attendant at a store. She was proud of her "Gift," who was able to accomplish information gathering - at such a young age.

They say we learn the best and fastest when we're very young; I would have to say that I was a good example. My skills at speaking, reasoning, evaluating, and calculating were rooted squarely in those precious years in my life before I ever started attending public school. Later, when my sister would join us at the dinner table and Dad would return home, we would argue cases before "The Judge," whether family squabble, school issue, or public policy. We debated a lot when I was a child. My father had been tutored in that art of persuasion and later became the debate coach at the local college, now Pitt University. At times, I look back, at my early tutelage and smile. No, I would not be where I am today without it.

Fuges as family of three

Grammies as a child at home by chicken coop

CHAPTER THREE
Emancipation Proclamation

My mother, it seemed to me, always thrived in the concrete jungle of downtown Pittsburgh. She took on its challenges and dangers fearlessly, with nothing but a walking cane for the blind in hand. She spent nearly ten years living and working within its complex collection of intertwining streets, odd-shaped buildings, trolley car tracks and busy intersections. As we were growing up, I always said that green carpeting was too much nature for Mom.

Mom had grown up on a slip of land on the edge of a mining community, the third of six children. Her father worked hard to support them all, both in the mines and collecting from a local orchard fruits, nuts and wild game. Their tiny homestead included an outdoor water pump, which fascinated me in my youth, and a small creek at the end of the property where raw sewage drained from the local homes. They supplemented nourishment for the family with a busy garden and the proceeds of their chicken coop. Dorothy Mae, ("Dot," as she was called), lost her vision before she started school from a childhood meningitis we can prevent now. She was thought to be the lucky one in their town as three children had been struck with this terrible infirmity. One died, one was left near a vegetable, and she "only" lost her vision.

She started her great adventure into Pittsburgh as a young girl, because she could get an excellent education at the well-known school for the blind. That school was not a pleasant place in the 1930s, but the school was still an avenue to accomplish for her, what her father had not been afforded—an education. He had started to work in the mines by the age of six. The Red Cross loaned the family the money for the required list of clothing and school supplies to get her enrolled for kindergarten. This wisp of a girl went reluctantly off to boarding school for the next dozen years.

On graduation, she went to business school and became an exemplary typist, learned to travel with a cane in unfamiliar and difficult environments, and ended up sharing a small apartment in downtown Pittsburgh. Dot worked as a stenographer for the Western Pennsylvania Psychiatric Hospital physicians. She always felt she had to work twice as hard to get half as far. Her lack of vision would keep her from any promotion. In the nearly ten years from her graduation, until she married, Dot did not receive a single increase in pay.

Dot did have an "in" with the girls at the office. Typewriters of that day did not have the pop out/pop in simple ink cartridges. They had a ribbon of ink wound on a spool that had to be threaded through parts of the heavy manual typewriter onto a spool on the other end. It could not be loose. It could not be too tight. It could not be wrinkled or twisted, and, if you got ink on your fingers, anything you touched throughout the rest of the day would have smudged fingerprints, as if you were a criminal leaving evidence of a crime. Never having done this particular process myself, I liken it to threading a bobbin through one of the more complicated sewing machines. Most of the ladies in the typing pool there either did not know how, or found it too difficult or too distressing to thread the ink ribbon. Mom was good at it. She made that complex process of feeding ribbon look easy.

Mom was perhaps not as appreciated for her typing as she could have been—not, that is, until just before she left work, when they did a time study. She was doing the second highest volume of work in the entire institution. She was appreciated for her acute hearing. Rather than the cassette tapes, on which I did the initial dictation for these stories, the dictations from the clinicians were cut onto wax rings that then had to be played back. The wax recordings were often muffled and difficult to understand, either from the process or the lack of clear speaking by the dictator. I remember growing up, having my parents drill into me to talk loudly, clearly, plainly and carefully. "Project and enunciate!" I wonder if it came from those days of struggling over faint, mumbled medical words.

Mom was to be married in 1958. To entice her not to leave her position at that time, Western Psych offered her her first real raise. The Emancipation Proclamation of The United States of America is famous because that is when Lincoln freed the slaves. Mom told us that her Emancipation Proclamation was her letter of resignation. She left that decade of life in the city to start over with L.H. Fuge, my Dad, in the mill town where he grew up, as Mrs. D.M. Fuge.

Grandpap, LHF and Grandma Nancy

CHAPTER FOUR
If She Can Do It, I Can Do It

Grandpap Fuge worked hard in a local mill, not an easy way to make a living for a family. He wasn't a big man, but he was a happy one. He always had a little crooked smile. Grandpap enjoyed teasing, so much so, he would stick his tongue out—especially for pictures, like his fiftieth wedding anniversary. I've been told that no one was happier than he, when my parents found that they were expecting their first child—which would turn out to be me. Grandpap Fuge walked often the short distance from where he and Grandma Nancy lived, to the old apartment above the Clairton business district, where my folks had their first home.

My grandparents didn't talk much about medical things or hardships or even happy times. They were stoic and quiet people. During that happy time while mom was pregnant with me, Grandpap Fuge had a devastating stroke. He was paralyzed on one side, left with no feeling in his hand, arm, leg, or foot, and certainly no mobility to walk. Now, Grandma Nancy was nothing if not an excellent nurse, having raise all those children without any outside health care. "If you couldn't take care of it yourself, it didn't get done," she used to say. I have no doubt that she tended to Grandpap's bodily needs quietly and efficiently.

A superb baker and excellent cook, Grandma Nancy went to work at the local school, in the cafeteria. She probably made millions of pies before it was all said and done. She was instructed to cut the pies when they were practically piping hot, to be able to have them ready for the kids as they came through. Grandma Nancy learned how to do an odd cut, some weird number, like 10 or 11 to be able to make more pieces per pie. It brought in needed money, because if you didn't go to work at the mill, you didn't get paid. If, there wasn't money, you didn't eat.

The happy event occurred. The gift of the bouncing baby girl my parents wanted arrived almost on schedule. The young blind couple had great joy in their life, but new responsibility. The two generations of adults were separated: Grandma Nancy and Grandpap Fuge, from the folks. The folks had moved a couple of blocks up the hill to their own first little house. For Grandpap Fuge, the distance must have seemed like miles. The story goes: Grandpap Fuge said, "If that baby can learn to walk, so can I." After his devastating stroke, he dragged himself, short distances at first, crawling when he needed to. Grandpap Fuge pushed himself a little bit, then a little bit more. Finally, slow and unsteady, he made the entire distance to visit me and our little family up the hill.

Eventually, he would rehab enough to be able to drive again. He never got feeling back in that hand or foot, and never talked about it, though he struggled. If he put his hand in his pocket, he never knew if there was something inside. He learned not to keep money on that side, because it could drop out on the floor, neither felt nor found. His persistence motivated me. Years later, when I would fight my way into medical school, I'd hear his words echoing in my ears: "Study hard." He didn't say much ever, but there was always his little crooked smile and determination to accomplish the near-impossible that drove me on. "If he can do it, I can do it."

Archibold, LHF and Grandma Nancy

CHAPTER FIVE
One Shot

Grandma Nancy was my dad's mother, born and raised in the Monongahela River Valley. Her family had been in this location for more than two hundred years. Our family had married into so many different nationalities and kinds of people over two centuries, that if folks asked if we were Italian or Slovak, English or Scotch-Irish, we could answer "Yes!" to each of them. Dad called our heritage "Heinz 57," after the local Heinz Factory. Heinz had initially come up with 57 varieties. As far as the family was concerned, he was teasing. Still, Dad could honestly say "yes" to just about *any* European nationality that you could name, and even Indian and African might be included somewhere over the many generations.

Grandma Nancy was sturdy stock, not a petite woman. She was always proper and restrained, not overly affectionate. Over the years, I slowly learned that she got so many of her strengths from her upbringing. It had not been an easy one. When Grandma Nancy was little, she was bounced out of a wagon and actually had her head run over by the wagon wheel. Miraculously, she lived with a cracked skull. She had damage to the mastoid, an area just behind the ear that can get infected and could be very dangerous to the brain. She managed to pull through, though her family didn't spend much money on medical care. They farmed a little piece of land. Her mother raised eleven children. To be more accurate, she gave birth to the children. Grandma, who was next to the oldest, got to do the work of raising them. From her telling, she was more of a servant to the family than a loved or coddled member. Grandma Nancy's home life made Psalm 27, verse 10 her favorite Bible verse. "When my father and my mother forsake me, then the Lord will take me up." From it all, she gained strength, drive and knowledge to help so many others later in life. Grandma Nancy's mother's name was Phoebe Laticia Hurl. Phoebe Laticia is where I got that wild streak that got me to live on a farm, city slicker that I was. I inherited my interest in riding and a love of horses from my great-grandmother, Phoebe.

She married Archibold McCleif Duff, another character. Phoebe spent her years having child after child, and trying to make ends meet at home. Archie would go on the road. He did transport jobs with horse and wagon. He would try to sell their chickens. Often, he was known for drinking, carousing, and fighting.

Times were hard in the Monongahela River Valley. Folks were trying to make ends meet where they could. There was one day when a couple of unscrupulous lads thought it might be easy pickings, as Mr. was away, to take food from the gardens that ran in front of the Duff home. The thugs were not distressed to see Phoebe Laticia standing on the front porch of the house down the lane.

A kid on one hip and another hanging off the other leg, is how I envision her. Surprised, not worried, she raised the firearm in her arms and sighted down the lane at them. "Best get out of there." They kept stealing the small harvest from the work that she had so diligently done in the garden with her children. Phoebe brought the firearm to her shoulder and fired. Bang! Down at the end of the lane, a shot landed just between the feet of the first garden thief. As Phoebe lowered the gun slightly, she bellowed down the lane, "Shells be expensive; won't waste another." I never forgot that image. We never heard another story of Phoebe Laticia having difficulty with thieves. Maybe the locals remembered the story as well as I did.

When Grandma Nancy passed away, my sister, Kid and I gave the eulogy, I remembered Phoebe again. I stood at the front of the funeral service, in the proud stance that I imagined Phoebe Laticia took and raised my arm as if to shoot. As I told the story, I smiled because "Grandma Nancy was at least that strong of will and spirit and body. If I have been fortunate enough to inherit some piece of that, I am truly blessed. Sometimes, you only get one shot at things."

Phoebe Laticia

**LHF as child (left) with her toy dog.
The blue poodle was not much of a watch dog,
it could make a good target.**

***Grammies (right) years later with Brandy.
The husky made an awesome watch dog until she died.**

CHAPTER SIX
Firearms Aren't Friendly

My father gave me my first exposure to firearms. I'm sure that decades later, fact and fiction, dreams, recollections, and reality have long since merged to make a fanciful story. What I know is that my father signed me up for Clairton Sportsman's Club. Dad was the one who showed me his firearms. He taught me respect for guns and an appreciation for beautiful and unique knives.

As a youth, I went to a local "Y" camp, up in the Laurel Mountains. I hated it; but there were a few positive experiences, one of which was going to a firing range. They had .22 caliber rifles, old single action. They weren't what you would call good quality. I can remember lying there prone, face down, looking down at the target, a stack of bullets beside me. We had to use a butter knife from the cafeteria to pry out the empty shell before putting in the new one—not what you would you call the proper way of handling a gun. I found that I was an excellent marksman.

The focus and solace helped me make a beautiful grouping on the target.

I envision Dad teaching respect for the power of firearms and ammunition in a kind of nightmare. Mother, more sensitive and cautious about such things, was appalled that we used the fireplace of their first home as a shooting gallery. There we shot a favorite stuffed animal, so I would always know that whatever was shot *never* came back. I can't recall which stuffed toy now, or the damage the ammunition did, but I will always know the concept that "firearms aren't friendly."

Imagination or distant fact? When I was six years old, we moved a block away to our new home. It had belonged to the Assistant Superintendent of the mill. There were seven fireplaces! There, all Dad's firearms were dismantled. The bolts and removable parts would be in two drawers on different floors. Three stories tall, plus an attic and basement, the house had ample space for the ammunition, in yet another location. To find all the parts to put one weapon together, two, three or four locations had to be searched. Neither children nor toys were in danger of accidental shootings in our home. I imagined if we were to be robbed, holding up a sign saying, "Please come back tomorrow. It's going to take me awhile to find some things."

When Clairton lost their local police force for the first time, my folks were living in their lovely home at the top of the hill with twenty-one huge windows. They were getting on in years. They no longer had a large dog living with them. Their children had moved away. For safety, Dad decided that, despite Mom's huge aversion to firearms, he would teach Mom how to shoot. He set up a firing range in the basement.

Dad himself, had been quite a marksman, having shot to sound. He hooked up a pulley system diagonally across their large, heavily-enforced basement. They would be able to shoot down towards the corner of the basement that had the extra coal cellar. On that pulley system, Dad put an empty gallon milk jug with wooden clothespins inside. The folks could stand down at one end, jiggle the pulley and make the milk jug jump. Clothespins bounced, making an audible target.

They were inventive and determined people, despite, or perhaps because of, their loss of sight.

I recall my mother using an iron. She put her bare hand at the hot point, using that to guide the iron, hour after hour, over the various folds and creases of my good dresses to keep them crisp, starched and wrinkle-free. No one would say she wasn't taking excellent care of her family, even without vision. I have emphatically called her extreme measures appalling. I don't have a word strong enough for the thought of my father, with no vision, teaching my mother, with no vision how to take the new cell phone, in case the phone lines were cut, and her firearm, into her safe hiding hole and to shoot if there was an intruder . . . let alone the two of them firing round after round for practice in that basement!

I told them that they should just let it be known at one of the little local bars in town that those crazy blind people on the hill have guns! They really wouldn't have to worry about someone breaking in. They wouldn't get mail maybe, but nobody would try to break in! I don't think they spoke to me for about a month after that conversation. I don't think they took my comments very kindly, but I remember well "firearms aren't friendly."

LHF and her Dad enjoy the deck of the Mount Summit Inn

CHAPTER SEVEN
Family Vacation

Cars must have been bigger in the past, or my family and I were much smaller. On family vacations, my mother, father, sister, grandparents and I all piled into Grandpap's Rambler. Four of us always sat in the back seat. Grandma rode in the passenger's seat up front, mostly to torment Grandpap. Grandpap drove. We kids were seated in the middle. I got carsick all the time. I'd have preferred a seat by a window for fresh air or to watch the scenery.

Pennsylvania has beautiful changing seasons and lovely mountains and valleys. I read that the Laurel Mountains, part of the Appalachian Mountains that ran through Pennsylvania, were more difficult to cross even than the Rocky Mountains, when the pioneers moved West. They did not seem so high. Maybe it was how steep they were. There was no snow on the top of the Laurel Mountains during the summer, like in pictures of the Rockies, but cooler, each year we beat the heat of the summer for three to eight days there.

Six of us piled into the Rambler. We drove from our little mill town along the Monongahela River, where the mills would make the air stinky, heavy, and dirty. We drove out the highway, further and further, until there were not any mills or factories or stores. The houses got further and further apart. Eventually, there were just trees on the steep sides of the Laurel Mountains. The Rambler didn't seem to want to go in those hot days, carrying the six of us and all the luggage that was the inevitable companion when my mother traveled. Certainly we couldn't have pushed the Rambler, but sometimes it seemed that we could have gotten out and walked faster. We climbed to the very top, to a hotel called the Mount Summit Inn.

A turn-of-the-century, frame building with multiple verandas welcomed you to Mount Summit Inn. There were sweeping staircases to the second and third floors. People would come out to the decks to visit on lounge chairs and watch the beautiful landscape. There were not a lot of recreational things to do in the Laurel Mountains, not even at the hotel. They did have an outdoor pool, with crisp, clear, albeit cool, refreshing water. These were the positive memories I had of swimming.

When we arrived at the Inn, I would go with Dad to check us all in at the desk. Grandpap would start unloading the dozen suitcases into piles. The piles were usually higher than my sister was tall. A petite girl, she was dwarfed by the size of the collection that we brought with us, even if we were just traveling for a few days. Good outfits for the evening dinner followed by music or dancing, long dresses, matching purses, shoes, shawls, jewelry, and fancy underwear. We brought long pants for the cool times out on the deck and shorts in case we got hot. Separate night outfits for each evening to lounge around in our rooms and, of course robes and slippers. Different shoes for each outfit, a trademark of my mother's, added to the volume.

Swimwear, coat, jacket, something in case it rained, the list of attire went on and on and on.

In addition to the clothes, we brought food. There were no convenience stores or fast food restaurants located along the road. The hotel had specific meal times, and you needed to arrive on time if you were going to get anything to eat. So we brought snacks; after all, we were traveling with children, children of *six* different ages, including two in their forties, and two in their sixties. There were fruits, crackers, cookies and cereals. Finally, there was a cooler for beverages and things that needed to be kept cold, like the five pounds of seedless grapes and the two baskets of strawberries. You might get the idea that we were a traveling caravan, except it all went in the one vehicle.

One of the nice things about this particular place to stay was that they had adjoining rooms. The adults could stay with a bedroom and a bathroom on one side and the children could stay with a bedroom and a bathroom on the other side. There was a door between the two. You didn't have to go out into the hallway of the hotel. We would leave the connecting door open, except during what we called "sleeping time." I figured out later, that's what my parents called it; when they wanted privacy, they shut the door. Then we knocked before we opened the door. Grandma Nancy and Grandpap would have a room on one side of us or just across the hall.

It was on one of these annual summer vacations that we figured out that my sister had exercise asthma. A band played one or two nights a week, mostly contemporary music. "Bridge Over Troubled Waters" was a particular favorite. They usually had some musician, probably twice our age, playing a drum or guitar or keyboard, whom Kid and I were trying to impress. Not that we were very good at dancing, but we gyrated endlessly for the entire time that he played. We moved as fast as possible, showing as much skin as we were able to in the attire that Mom had allowed.

It was an all-evening event whenever the band played—right up until Kid collapsed at the stage, short of breath and overheated. Of course, this was not the approved time for getting to the dining hall. Where would we be able to get ice? We were some distance away from the main hotel area where the one and only ice machine was housed for this large, ancient structure. Dad, ever ready, proceeded to feed the one-dollar bills he had with him into the pop machine, to get a huge pile of cold pop cans. We packed Kid in cans, cooled her down and calmed her breathing. The moral was: when you need help, always call for Dad. Dad can fix anything.

It never dawned on me that most fathers didn't carry around twenty ones in their wallets. With no vision, my father had learned to carry only two sizes of bills: fives, which he had flat in a billfold and ones, which he had folded over in a money clip. That way, if he gave somebody a bill and was expecting change, he always knew what the change was. It had to be ones. This night, having that many ones came in very handy.

On one such summer vacation, we went down to the pool, something akin to ice water. I was showing off my wonderful new bathing suit, a one-piece with a frilly skirt. Not exactly the perfect fit, but it was the only one I had. I had been desperate to get it. It was on the clearance rack at K-Mart, or a blue light special, and so, Mom acquiesced.

Dad was showing my sister and me how to sit on the side of the pool. Just lean forward into the water gently. No splashing and turning bright florescent red from a diving board. Hold your breath. Push off the side of the pool and go underwater for as far out as you can. Then come up for air. We were having a wonderful time playing around, learning these things with Dad.

I kept watch out of the corner of my eye to see if any of the interesting characters visiting at the hotel were watching us from one of the decks. Then, I got quite a lesson in what happens when you do not get clothes that fit just right—especially if you are planning on going in the water. What happened was the ballooney, frilly skirts that was the thing of the time, filled up with water and kind of blew up like a beach ball. The water and the extra frilly material, dragged on me, as I pushed off the side of the pool. As I headed down towards the deep end of the pool in my swimsuit that didn't fit quite tight enough, it started to slink down off the top half of my body. I screamed, "Help!"

Dad rushed to the rescue. He knew that his daughters did not really know how to swim. He had been quite the avid swimmer before he lost his vision as a teen. He was very happy that we were spending time in the water. He assumed that the catastrophe at hand was actually an emergency, not a clothing fiasco. He dived in to the sound of my voice, came up from underneath me, and threw me onto the deck of the pool, my bathing suit completely down, pretty much around my hips, mortified, naked, shivering, and furious. I learned never to call for "*help*" unless I really, really needed it, not even in prayer. My father went on to tell this story, even on the way to my wedding to Tom, still finding it immensely amusing decades later.

LHF as Department of Family Medicine Chairman
waits for a meeting at her renovated office. Decades later, she still
relaxes with her feet in the fifth ballet position.

CHAPTER EIGHT
Stand Up and Be Proud

Five feet tall by the time I was in kindergarten, I towered over my classmates. My teacher was very understanding about the fact that I still sucked my thumb, chocolate flavor on the left, we decided. She was more militant about the organization of her "troops" for activities. We needed to line up in order of size to go everywhere; the tallest, me, *always* last. I was last to lunch, last to bathroom breaks, last to pick out instruments for music and last for treat selection.

It was not long before I was trying to be shorter. I stooped. I slouched. I bent my knees and leaned—anything I could think of to move up closer to the front, obviously with limited success. My parents really began to worry as I slumped around the house. They encouraged me to stand up straight and be proud of my height. By first grade, with my posture not improved, they were sure that I needed professional help to figure out what to do with my lanky limbs.

Dance class was the local option. By seven years of age I was enrolled in ballet. Thin scraggly hair, uncertain, with huge feet, I was not the picture of poise and beauty. I tried. I stretched. The folks paid. Dozens of stretch pants were torn in my attempts to bounce into splits on the floor. Many were the people I tripped in hallways as I practiced the required ballet positions with my feet.

One flaw in the plan was that to do the second ballet position correctly, I needed to be able to turn my legs and hips out far to the side. I practiced standing with my feet turned out far to the right and left. When sitting, I would splay my knees out to the sides, looking something like a catcher squatting down ready to ambush a fast ball. I am not sure who was more distressed with this "unladylike" position, Mom or Grandma Nancy. Grandma Nancy would say "Good girls don't sit like that…they might get *pregnant.*" It was as if she thought sperm was floating in the air, waiting for some unsuspecting girl that did not have her legs crossed. I have pondered, if only Grandma Nancy had been right, maybe I would not have been adopting children later in life. I conformed, and am trained so well now that if I sit down, one knee almost automatically jumps up and crosses over the other. Medically, crossing legs at the knees is a problem for pulling backs out of alignment, increasing varicose veins and risk for blood clots, so I am trying to change my habits again.

Eight years of ballet classes and several recitals later, I stood every inch of five foot nine inches, erect and confident. I could prance onto the stage, or into the classroom with a commanding stride.

Little did we know then that I would be commanding attention in front of Board meetings and Medical Staffs in years to come.

More importantly, now, when I want to see eye-to-eye with someone, I take a better approach. I ask to sit on their bed in the hospital, I kneel down beside them or I share a hug.

**Sikira and LT study pumpkins and
their curly vines in the fields of our farm***

CHAPTER NINE
Art As A Gift

From my grade school, I was fortunate enough to be one of three school students selected for an art scholarship program to Carnegie Institute in Pittsburgh, Pennsylvania. From the 1940s through the 1980s, this program was run by a local artist, Mr. Fitzpatrick. Every week for some forty years, he lectured to hundreds of youths. His motto was: "To look, To see, To remember, To enjoy." He gave the gift of his time and talent to generations of Pennsylvania youths, as more than two hundred schools got to select candidates each year to attend free. We found out after we were married that Tom and I had both shared in Mr. Fitzpatrick's tutelage when we were growing up.

Chosen by the Director of Art for Clairton Public Schools, I was Blessed with three years of art education, simply because as a city-girl, I was observant enough to draw pumpkins with *curly* vines. All I had to do was take two buses before seven in the morning to get there.

Each week, we wrote Mr. Fitzpatrick's motto and submitted a two-sided assignment. One side was calligraphy, the other colored sketches. In three years, my colored side made high honors only once, but the third year, my calligraphy side won honors every week! Because of that distinction, I earned an extra two years of art scholarship, which included painting. I have never learned to be a good painter, but for that gift of *another* two years of Mr. Fitzpatrick's mentoring, I will always be grateful.

While I will never be an artist, those five years gave me a huge appreciation for the arts. Though decades in medicine and arthritis in my hands have taken my penmanship, my love of creativity remains. Whenever I have been under stress, I have found it rejuvenating to seek an artistic outlet. During high school, when there was a long break from school because of terrible winter storms, I crocheted afghans. The first one was done with just scraps of white yarn from around the house. That was when I learned that you had to buy *all* of the yarn for a project at one time. That initial project ended up as many different shades of white and needed to be dyed before it looked good enough to be used. Made of several different stitches, it made a unique gift for my daughter, as she was losing her eyesight.

Homesick, away at college, I thought I would try making a hook rug. The backing material was cheaper to buy plain. Kits with pre-drawn picture outlines already on them were ten dollars for a one foot by two feet design. The backing material was only three dollars a yard. "Give me five yards," I requested, now, I was thinking of feet. As the sales person began to reel off length after length of the stuff, I stopped her at about nine feet, or just over three yards. It took me a very long time to finish my rug. Gifted for Christmas to my family, it hung on one wall in my parents' forty foot living room for more than twenty-eight years, until it was sold in their estate sale.

Medical school was some of the worst time in my life. For my outlet there, I did a version of Joseph's multi-colored coat. Using fabric scraps from hundreds of old sewing projects of my family, I cut out thousands of three-inch hexagons. From them I hand-sewed flowers with three rows of petals each. Putting strips together of complimentary colors made a rainbow of rows: two each of pinks, purples, blues, greens, yellows, and oranges. One central row of reds completed my "garden" quilt. Each flower held a different memory. This one a halter; that one, a baby's blanket; the next, a holiday vest. Each item had its own unique texture as well—a perfect way, I thought, for my two blind parents to be able to distinguish among the flowers. My plan was to give it to my parents for their twenty-fifth anniversary. Unfortunately, Dad was raised by Grandma Nancy to believe that every piece for a quilt must match perfectly in texture, age, and if possible, size. That way, the quilt would age evenly. No one part would wear out faster than another. Hearing that, I got new, big six by six-inch calico squares, sewed them all together by machine and had a quick, but acceptable gift for their wedding anniversary.

Scrapbooking has taken the place of more challenging handmade items today. I can do as little as one page or picture at a time, if my hands are not up to more. Though family and a few privileged friends have gushed over my attempts at artistic, handmade gifts, I know that truly, I am the one that has received joy and contentment through creativity.

**LHF and two-wheeler
between the bush and sidewalk at the back of house**

CHAPTER TEN
Staying on the Path

I was one of those fortunate children whose parents did everything they could to make sure that I was happy. You could not say that I had everything I ever wanted, but I certainly lacked for nothing.

One of the essentials of growing up, in my parents' eyes, was a bicycle. Elbow pads and knee pads were not used then. We would ride on public streets, go careening down hills, do one-leg stands off the pedal on the side of the bike, or balance off of the handle bars. The mandatory biking helmet of today was not even considered. Value was a concern so we went to a Schwinn bike store for great quality. They measured how tall I was. We checked out the brakes. My clothes may have been bought at K-Mart, but this, the first thing I would drive, would be top-of-the-line.

I am not sure how we got the monster home. I was a very tall youngster and my first two-wheeler was too. It seemed to materialize at the end of our sidewalk at 446 Mitchell Avenue. We had a narrow path of concrete from the street to our back porch, barely fifty feet long with the house on the left, and a hill on the right. It seemed like a marathon.

I did not have a clue how to balance on those little, skinny wheels. My father had not lost his vision until he was a teenager, so he had certainly done bicycling himself. He took it upon himself to teach me the fundamentals of keeping the bike on that path. He stood on the pedals. Holding on tight to the handle bars, steadily, slowly, he started down the narrow path towards our back door. He probably made twenty or thirty feet before he rolled off the walk into the forsythia bush. We kids certainly did not laugh, funny a sight as it must have been; this was serious business. With his guidance, I managed to master first that path, and then the street. I even tried a number of dare-devil maneuvers that would be scoffed at by today's acrobatic trail bikers. Dad's lessons of staying on the path, getting up when you fall and continuing to try even when it seems impossible would be a godsend for my future. Some paths just have more twists, turns and bumps than others.

LHF sits on Mom's red Lincoln just down from the garage

CHAPTER ELEVEN
A Matter of Physics

A number of interesting moments in my life have to do with driving. Curiously enough, many involved my father, despite his not having driven in many years. Dad had learned to drive by the age of thirteen, but during my lifetime, Dad had no vision.

Mom, my avid shopping, travel companion, started me on the road to becoming a driver when I turned fifteen. She was going to get a car. It would be *her* vehicle. Her favorite color was red, she reminded us all. She had been saving for a *long* time.

We went from location to location hunting a vehicle. Sometimes people took us to car dealerships in their vehicles and waited patiently. Sometimes, we walked. We even took the bus, as it was our usual mode of transportation. At each dealership, Mom was very clear on her criteria. We needed a four-door vehicle, red preferably—not orange or brown—with an enormous trunk. A hapless salesman took us to the very first vehicle, a bright orange two-door sports car. He got no second try. Hunting for vehicles was frustrating. For awhile, we wondered who was the visually impaired – us or the dealers.

Finally, at the Lincoln Mercury dealership, on Route 51, heading towards Pittsburgh, we found an enormous red Lincoln Towne Car. From behind the wheel, you could look over the end of the vehicle many, many, many feet in front of you, with a feeling of invincibility. My dad often teased that this was as close to a tank as he was legally allowed to put onto the highways and it got about the same gas mileage.

Our "red boat," as we nicknamed it, had an enormous trunk. Mom had Dad get inside to "see." All her luggage would fit, six pieces per person, he assured her. Oh, she was proud of her vehicle! Once I got my license, she would consider allowing me to drive it with permission, presumably to take her somewhere. It was not a recreational vehicle for me; it was transportation for the family and it belonged to Mom.

Our home had a free-standing garage built of concrete block big enough for at least two vehicles. There was an enormous amount of storage space around where the vehicles would sit inside. The short little driveway that came out of the garage was perpendicular to the street. My dad had the bright idea that I should learn how to back out of the garage and onto the street, as soon as we got the car. That way, when I finally had a driver's license, this would already be easy.

I had not had his youthful opportunities to practice driving go-karts or tractors. I would need direction. So, he measured the garage. He measured the driveway, proudly pacing it off, one step at a time, as was his custom, and knowledgeably stretching his arms the six feet that his reach spanned for the garage and vehicle measurements.

Dad made it all into a wonderful math problem. He was so proud of physics. He used those calculations to see exactly how many turns of the steering wheel it would take to back the vehicle out. Swinging out the short drive and onto the road was the plan, me behind the wheel, Dad beside me, explaining it all. "Look behind you. Watch where you're going. Make sure there's no vehicle coming up on the street." He explained which direction I should turn the wheel. He calculated that exactly three and one-fourth turns of the steering wheel would maneuver the vehicle out onto the highway. "Go slowly," he advised "Allow time for the vehicle to slowly turn."

All was well with the plan. I learned to turn the car on. We covered watching the rearview mirror. I learned the seat adjustments. (Seat belts were not quite so much the thing back then.) I looked for traffic. We checked to see that there was nothing on the ground in the driveway to bother the tires. We did everything but spit-polish the shine on the vehicle.

Finally, we started out. One steering wheel turn . . . CRUNCH! I hit the side of the stone garage door with the front left fender of my mother's brand-new, bright red Lincoln Towne Car! Oh, Dad was furious! So angry! "You weren't paying attention. You weren't counting. You were going too fast. What were you doing?" Many tears later, and quite a repair bill, we figured it out. When Dad had learned to drive, they didn't have something called *power steering*. He had needed to fight the steering wheel around quite a number of times with a good bit of effort to make the front of such a large vehicle turn. With wonderful power steering and just a smooth little turn of the wheel, as I looked dutifully behind me for traffic I spun the front of that vehicle around SPLAT! right into the wall, even denting the great heavy metal. Now Dad, who was always fond of saying, "It's a matter of physics," had one more example—just not one he was particularly fond of.

Later in life, when Tom and I would move to Promises Kept Farm, we needed to get a large truck to be able to make it in and out of the rough farm roads. To haul water and other extremely heavy loads, we were looking at a one-ton, eight-foot bed, enormous vehicle. The salesman teased me that I would need forty acres to turn it around. I smiled to myself because, after all, our farm was forty acres. I asked him, slyly, "It depends. Does it have power steering?"

LT enjoys shoveling stables*

CHAPTER TWELVE
"Stupid Shovel"

Mom's dad was named after a little town in France just outside of Lourdes. Like so many that came to settle the small mining community in Washington County, he had little formal education. Pap-pap started working in the mines at six years of age, straddling a conveyor belt as the pieces of coal moved from where they were dug out, into a train car. His job was to pick out the debris called shale. He spent his young life supporting his family from any mining job he could get.

Despite his limited learning, Pap-pap enjoyed reading. I remember fondly getting him books by Louis L'Amour. American westerns were his favorite. Maybe my love of reading came from him. He always said, "Dogs don't have cats." In his seventies, he was elected County Commissioner. Pap-pap spoke to all of the property owners in their local communities to get the easements of land needed to finish their local road system. Intolerant of inactivity despite his advanced years, he often went out with the road crews, mostly young kids on summer jobs, many decades younger than himself. His years in the mines had taught him some useful skills. He could have had a doctorate in the physics and anatomy of shoveling. He was known to jump on the back of a truck, with the road crew, to show the kids how to shovel properly so that they would be more efficient and not get injured.

On a visit with my parents, my father went out to shovel snow and Pap-pap went with him. He admonished my father to let the shovel do the work. After loading ton after ton of heavy coke ore, the snow must have seemed light to Pap-pap. Dad would hold out the snow shovel at arm's length, a much lighter weight tool than Pap-pap used for coal. My Dad would tease Pap-pap that he got a "stupid shovel." It does not know what it is doing.

Even into his eighties, dying from black lung, a disease contracted from the years of breathing the coal dust, we grandchildren would give Pap-pap a wide berth. If we were running through the house, he was quick to reach out his arm and grab you. Pap-pap's hands still had the strength of steel itself, a grip honed by a lifetime of hard labor.

My mother was his darling and he managed to get her an excellent education. I think perhaps he was also proud of her husband, the attorney, who would not have to make their living by relying on the intelligence and strength of a stupid coal shovel.

**Mayor L. H. Fuge* runs the City Council
and LaDonna builds a campfire**

CHAPTER THIRTEEN
Prepared For The Rescue

Girl Scouts met at our local Church. It was an avenue to get me some safe interaction with girls my own age, close to home.

Most of the local families were blue collar, working families. This distinction was said with pride. "Work" was the operative word. Mill workers labored in extreme conditions to support their loved ones. Some worked as machinists, mechanics, or in glass making. The service industries included our local Police and Fire Departments, Street Maintenance and Garbage Collection, Teachers and Preachers. Clairton had a small business district with individually-owned shops, a laundry, a fruit market, a hardware store and shoe repairs. Because its local government was run by a mayor, Pennsylvania categorized Clairton as a "city." At one time, it had a population of some 25,000.

My sister and I did not fit in easily. There were three doctors, a dentist, and three or four attorneys. A couple of the professionals went on into politics. Our family was in this last group—a segregated bunch. Interactions on the campaign trail were rarely conducive to forming good friendships, as candidates fought hard for personal victory. We were viewed as the "spoiled rich kids with the blind parents from that big house." "They think they are better than everyone else," because their Mom was the President of the Women's Club and the PTA; she also was a presenter at the Public Library Book Club and led philanthropic events. Worse, their Dad was an attorney and Mayor!

Scouts was a rare occasion to mingle. Plus, we got to do "neat" things, like study how to make campfires or cloth dolls, and learn how to ride horses or cook. Animosity did not completely dissolve when we donned that green uniform. There were still one or two individuals who persisted in teasing me about everything from my K-Mart clothes, to how I walked—even that I spoke clearly and distinctly with big, fancy words.

One of the mottos of the Girl Scouts is to "be prepared." So I was really just following the rules when an opportunity came up to teach my worst tormentor a lesson. I had read the First Aid manual before our weekly meeting. I was not sure how I would tear a forty by forty-inch swatch out of my slip to make a sling or tourniquet as the text directed, since our entire outfits did not have that much material— but I was prepared to do a rescue.

As usual, my lead tormentor was first to volunteer to the Troop Leader. That day, I was next. "That's okay; *you* can lie down on the blanket. I will do the work part, and pretend to rescue you from the burning building . . ." I crooned. Pretending to jump in through a window to where our "victim" lay overcome with smoke, I unceremoniously flipped her onto her back onto a blanket. Just as the book had directed, I made a big show of folding the two top corners over her face, "to protect her." Meanwhile, I caught huge handfuls of hair into the folds of material, all the while yelling, "Don't cry" and "I'll save you." With all my might, I pulled her hard and fast, by her hair and that blanket, the length of the floor. All the while, she was screaming. The troop thought she was a great role-player. Out the door and down the short flight of steps, head first. Bump, bump, thump, she hit her head off each tread as we went down.

The Troop Leader seemed well pleased with my "performance." For her part, my tormentor left me alone after that. I was, obviously, "crazy and dangerous!" For my part, I never enjoyed earning a merit badge more. Happily, since then, I have studied healing and taken an oath to "do no harm."

Grandma Nancy as a girl in the Monongahela River Valley

CHAPTER FOURTEEN
The God Squad

The clearest picture in my memories of Grandma Nancy is when she was in her eighties, perhaps because this is the most recent, or perhaps because she always had a very mature, stoic, even formidable look for most, if not all, of my life. The God Squad is evidence that she had been young once. When she was a young girl, she started going to Bible School with other young girls in the community. They studied, prayed and read the Bible. What is unique is that this group of eight girls continued their Bible Class each week into their eighties. They shared eight decades of devotion and prayer, believing in the power of divine intervention.

My grandfather spent much of his time in his garden,

which was more flowers than food. I envision him always outside; but Grandma Nancy spent all of her time in her little kitchen. She was a great baker. There was one tiny window in the back wall of her kitchen. It was just big enough to let in a breath of air or catch a view of a bird that had come to settle on her plum tree. That tree blocked almost all the view but produced beautiful fruit. I imagined how wonderful it must be for Grandma Nancy, baking in her kitchen and talking conversationally with her Lord each day in prayer. In my child's mind I pictured her opening her window saying "Excuse me, Sir. When you have a minute..." As an adult, I was impressed with the quiet peace Grandma Nancy's Faith gave her.

Sad in her youth, Grandma Nancy had turned to her Bible.When she died, we found in her Bible the testament that she had penned with her young hand, the testament that saved her. She spoke of her difficult life. Often she had prayed, "Yea, though I walk through the valley of death, I will fear no evil for Thou art with me." In her distress, those words did not move her. They did not catch her soul. Then she found the passage, "Though your mother and father forsake you, I will not" and it lifted her spirit and saved her. She was never again alone. So powerful and sincere was her devotion that I could hardly imagine anything the Lord would deny her, that she lifted up to Him in prayer.

I imagined the awesome depth and power of the connection between her group of sincere and devout women praying together. Perhaps I was a little afraid of the "God Squad"— my name for them, not theirs; but, I respected them. Any number of crises in my young life, I would turn to our Lord in prayer through them.

**Mom's red Lincoln wrapped in blue crepe paper
for high school graduation***

CHAPTER FIFTEEN
The Seed is Planted

When I became an adult, the story of my education was somewhat different than it had been during my earliest years. When I came home from college or medical school for the holidays and Grandma Nancy, who eventually lived with my folks, would greet me, it was with a different type of comment than when I was a bald, chubby infant. "Brilliant," was only a distant echo. "Fat," she'd say matter-of-factly, "you're getting fat." I'd try to ignore her or calmly reply, "Nice to see you too, Grandma."

The folks and I'd converse, over a snack around the table, about my challenge of the moment: biochemistry, zoology, calculus. Grandma Nancy would "tsk, tsk," shake her head, look at the floor and sigh, "If only you had your father's brains, dear." I was sure she meant it. When I was in the best of moods, I could agree. I'd smile and say, "Me, too, Grandma. It would make my life a lot easier."

In fact, my life had been easy in many ways, thanks to the strong foundation of early years my folks had laid. Kindergarten through sixth grade were spent at the local public school. The pace of the general classroom was ploddingly slow. I supplemented my school day with reading dozens of paperbacks. Scholastic's book program offered a new collection of paperbacks each month. My folks allowed me to buy every book offered. I pursued an eclectic combination of topics. I learned about motorcycles and hot rods, nature and travel, mysteries and romances, fiction and history. This early love of reading and the extreme breadth of topics perhaps made me a more well-rounded person.

My folks saved for everything. My books, my education, even our home. They bought our first house, at 434 Halcomb with a down payment of fifty-cent pieces. In those days, a bus ride to Pittsburgh was fifty cents. Dad would pay his dollar, for the trip and get a fifty-cent piece change. Every ride, he would save. The sacrifice of no lunch or snack put savings into a precious nest egg for the future. Even when they were engaged, my parents only spent the extra bus fare to visit each other once a week. Their moments together were extra precious, because they were so scarce. Eventually, hundreds of chubby fifty-cent pieces made up their down payment.

When I was thirteen, there was an extended strike in the Clairton public schools. My sister and I made the fateful trip by bus to an aggressively academic parochial school, St. Elizabeth's. I nearly flunked the first semester; their sprint-like pace was a huge shock. They were doing algebra; I was lost. I struggled for the first time ever in school. The nuns were attentive, persistent and interested in stimulating creativity. By the end of eighth grade, I caught up with my academically-motivated peers. Advanced reading, mathematics, history and science had a dozen of us pushing towards college. With them, I obtained the foundation that would make my path to becoming a physician a reality.

The academic students all seemed to get braces at that time. Rather than let it be a subject for teasing, we proudly declared it was a clear sign of the "intelligentsia." We were stuck up.

By the time I was thirteen, my parents explained that either I would select a course of education to pursue or they would enroll me in one! I was adamant that I would go into family practice.

I don't know if today's Family Practice was even available then. But I had had a good family doctor in our community. Just as importantly, I had had a bad hospital experience. My family's way of helping me cope with that was to say, "Isn't it a shame that they didn't have more of those good family doctors to help out those poor hospital doctors who needed it so badly?" The seed had been planted.

LHF graduates from High School with honors

CHAPTER SIXTEEN
Matriculation

My father had many honors in college. He graduated summa cum laude from Pitt. Dad went on to their law school. Phi Beta Kappa, an honor-based fraternity, was one of his accomplishments.

Growing up, his Sigma Chi fraternity brothers and our family socialized. They were an eclectic group. Dad, an attorney, and Mayor. Dad's debate partner, Bud Schuster, a fraternity brother, became a U.S. Congressman from our state. Joe Marasco founded a radiology group in the community. Joe went on to national honors in his field, finally retiring to be Medical Director of the community hospital in Monroeville, called Forbes. To me, the most important member of the Sigma Chi brothers' fraternity was a quiet, high school counselor by the name of Ed Bash. Ed worked in a large public school system called Jefferson, near our home.

The Bashes were an interesting family. Ed and his brother, Ted, married two of three sisters. Ed and his wife lived out in a small community on the edge of Clairton with Dorothy, the third sister and her husband living down the lane. Ed built a little barn there. My dad helped him. The Bashes had horses and daughters. The Bashes and the Fuges shared dreams of educating their daughters. Patty, their oldest, just a couple of years ahead of me, would become a Vet.

Mr. Bash helped me solidify my dream of becoming a physician, still not that common for women in those days. We searched out educational options around the state and across the country, like we were on a treasure hunt or tracking a rainbow for some pot of gold. My father's alma mater was eventually excluded from that search because they did not have family medicine as an option in their medical school. We toured different places. We got statistics about their getting their graduates admitted to medical school. We considered the time commitment and academic agenda. Finances were a distant third on the list of criteria. Thomas Jefferson and Penn State were considered along with smaller, private schools.

I took PSATs early. The SATs are usually done in the last years of high school, but the PSATs can be earlier. My score on them was high enough for me to qualify for a scholarship based on the score. That is, if I left for college in my sophomore year. The folks were not planning on having me jump out of high school and onto that dream so early. My impatience prompted me to consider it, but the thought of leaving home terrified me.

When it did come time to take SATs, I had not studied at all. I had not needed to study throughout high school. Information seemed to come easily. French was my sole stumbling block. Geometry, physics, even calculus were not big challenges, only stepping stones.

My biology teacher, crazy Mary Schmidt, I remember affectionately. She motivated a love of research, investigation, analysis and science. Brownie points were given for wild experiments and collection of field research and dissection, things like worms or frogs. Never again did I get a simply "satisfactory" science grade.

I enjoyed my weeks in her classroom and my weekends touring academia, looking for a spot for my future. With Ed Bash's help, we settled on Gannon, a little diocesan school in Erie, maybe three hours away, with a 98% acceptance rate to medical school for those who completed their undergraduate program. Later in life, I'd learn to listen carefully to *each* word included in the statement, like that word "completed." The unstated fact was that more than 50% would flunk out, change majors or leave. Still, Gannon had an awesome program. For an undergraduate, it included an electron microscope, human cadaver dissections, live theater studies, and a chance to travel in Europe for summer semesters. Academic, service, and athletic fraternities and service groups were all available. Small when compared to Penn State, the individual attention lavished upon their students was special. Each student was known by name and by sight. Their dreams were a matter of individual concern for the professors in such small classes. The entire school had maybe three thousand students, including those attending night classes.

Individuality and Academics – and so it was decided. The 70s would end with me studying at Gannon College. Not just Pre-Med, but a Bachelor of Science Degree in Family Medicine from what would become Gannon University. Situated in Erie, Pennsylvania, small town in its feel, though third largest city in the state by size. My voracious appetite for knowledge and my impatience for acquiring my dream served me well in those months away from home on the next step of my life's path.

St. Elizabeth's graduated me with all the pomp and fanfare of a parade down the aisle of the large church. Cap, gown and gold braid, I accomplished only sixth in my class because they included those in business classes along with those of us in academics. The grade point averages, for those seemingly lesser classes, had "mere" business majors graduating second, third, and fourth place in our class. I only got one gold tassel instead of two because of those three business majors ahead of me. Still, I matriculated proudly to my next level of education.

LHF and Mom at High School graduation

Universidad Maria Christina,
at the monastery of San Lorenzo Del Escorial, Spain,
where LHF studied with a college group from Gannon.
Living quarters were in the square, front and center.

CHAPTER SEVENTEEN
Joining In

Growing up, I lived within two blocks of four churches and four funeral homes. At one point, one of the funeral homes was actually converted into a church. My dad always said that "none of us would get out of here alive" and "we would be no different." Now, as a Christian, I know that if we believe, we are going to a better place. However, my medical training has me fighting against Death as a determined foe. As a physician, I do not go to funerals if I can help it; it seems an acknowledgement that my adversary has won.

My parents did not raise us in any particular religion. We were not baptized. Dad had gone onto postgraduate education in Philosophy after Law School. He had a great interest in the world's religions and exposed us to a plethora of options. It was left up to each of us to decide for ourselves what we would believe in, practice and join as adults.

We grew up going to Bible school at the United Presbyterian Church across the street. Summers were spent at their Church camp activities. Grandma Nancy belonged to the United Methodist Church. We were included in their family events through her. Dad appreciated any religion based on "The Golden Rule." His teaching and studying included Muslim, Buddhist, Shinto, and a range of Judeo-Christian sects. Before my sister and I started to attend St. Elizabeth School, we had already been in Temple, Mosque and Synagogue.

I did not feel isolated or lost. To the contrary, I was welcomed wherever I went to worship. There was a revival meeting one summer across the street and I joined in the praising and singing. Uplifting and euphoric sensations stayed with me for some time following.

When a self-proclaimed minister of a small, non-denominational church took over a local funeral home for youth meetings, I decided to go with one of my neighborhood teen acquaintances. It never occurred to me to worry about cults or our safety.

We were welcomed. We were given refreshments and placed into a circle to pray. That was when it started getting out of hand for me. Some of the young adults started making odd noises. Some fell to the floor and writhed around. Others were swaying back and forth. I was shaken up. Scared, rather than uplifted, I rocked back and forth. I could hear myself saying, "Oh my God, oh my God, oh my God." Maybe they thought I was joining in. Me, I was looking for the door! That single experience probably put me off joining a church for some time.

Years later, when I was studying for two semesters in Europe, I got a chance to see up close the enormous

Cathedrals of several countries. The beauty, majesty and power of will that were captured in their poetic structures were awe-inspiring. I made a solo pilgrimage to Fatima in Portugal, and took a group of fellow students on an excursion to Lourdes, France. When I returned home to the United States, I was baptized Christian.

Faith has sustained me through life, Medical School and my career's war against illness, disease and grief. I have come to believe and often said that, "There should be no atheists in foxholes or medical schools." Both are hostile environments, where death can surprise you around any corner. Faith comforts me with the knowledge that we are not in this alone.

*Valley of the Fallen's cross in Spain stands nearly 500 feet tall. This 1970's photo by Dr. Fuge was the inspiration for the cover.

**LHF lived in the Allegheny National Forest
to earn extra science credits**

CHAPTER EIGHTEEN
The Rest is History

Over the years, I've said that I had changed high schools so that I wouldn't have to take swimming at Clairton Public School, where all the girls had to shower together in a large common shower. Whether that was a reflection of the bad memories of the swim classes in that same pool with Mac or some false sense of modesty, I don't know. I say false sense of modesty because being raised by blind parents made for an odd appreciation of nudity.

My father had no vision at all. There was no concern about him "seeing" his daughters, as they matured into adolescence and became women, walking with or without clothes from the living room or bathroom. Many times we had our family discussions in the bathroom between my sister's room and mine. One of us using the toilet, the other in the tub, my mother beside the little heater in the bathroom. She was always cold. Dad would be sitting in the open doorway. We talked about the plans for the week or hopes for the future, anything and nothing. Despite this seeming communal upbringing, the concept of the community shower just didn't sit well with me. With no such gym activity, I was ready to move from St. Elizabeth's eighth grade, all the way across their driveway, to St. Elizabeth High School.

Frighteningly, there was a brief moment when I thought we might return to Clairton for school. The unrest was settled. The strike was over. My father was Mayor of Clairton at that time. Dad was inaugurated in January, 1973, for a four-year term that would stretch through much of my school years. Swimming, gym and showers not withstanding, there was not any real consideration for resuming public education. My feet were firmly set on the path towards a professional future.

Perhaps I was a disappointment for not staying in Law. I often said I would do both Medicine and Law, as Dad's classmate, Cyril Wecht, had done.

When I leaf back through memories and memorabilia of those high school years, I remember my odd collection of academic friends. A few of those many names stand out after more than thirty years, each brilliant in his or her own way. It's funny how different, unique characters come to mind. Rita was going on to study United States, political and Russian relations, probably work in D.C. or the Secret Service or Europe. Helen Marie was from my home town. A pleasant family, they had a large camper trailer in their driveway. I imagined them touring, vacationing across our great country. Donna, soft-spoken, quiet, could easily have been a nun, for as gracious and sweet was her temperament. Janet, one of eight or nine children in her family, I imagine having escaped into life as an engineer or some other profession before raising a family of her own. Bernie loved music. His family wanted him to study business. Chris, who taught me how to cut a deck of cards with one hand, ran the little local gambling pool on whatever sporting event was in the news of the day. He was brilliant at the lighting of our high school drama productions. We each had our own niche and reason to get good grades.

Math presented a problem with that. The nun in charge of that class was formidable. A fair-sized woman, she tolerated no disruption, noise, or fluttering of papers in her classroom. I can remember stifling a cough, almost choking myself rather than making noise—and having her stride firmly down the aisle towards me. I had no idea what my fate would be for disrupting her Geometry tutelage. She glared down at me . . . placed a cough drop on my desk.

Sr. John the Baptist had an interesting view of math grading for her class. Parent/teacher conferences at our high school set aside time to meet with any of the dozen instructors in one evening. There were only a moderate number of parents. Folks would usually pick the classes where they had the most interest or concern for their child. I had only received a "B" in geometry from her, despite a perfect score on all papers.

My mother, five feet in heels and a hairdo, and one hundred pounds of concrete, stormed in to the presence of the matriarch of the math room to confront her about the discrepancy. Mom was greeted with, "What are you doing here? I don't need to see you!"

Mom's reply: "I need to see you! What's the meaning of a "B" for these scores?" Although not present for the explanation, I've been told that Sister John the Baptist explained that there were six students with equal scores. She could only give one A+, one A, one A-, and two B+s; and the rest had to be B or below. Since boys would need their education more, my friends Bernie and Chris had gotten the higher grades.

My mother was appalled and explained she "would have her head on a platter" if we had that type of nonsense ever again. Grades were to reflect the appropriate level of effort and accomplishment, regardless of background or gender. There were no more problems with math grades.

Sister Claire was another matter. Rita excelled at languages. She spoke beautifully in Spanish and went on to do equally well in French. Not me. Sister Claire, who taught language, was a wisp of a woman whom we called "snake." Her eyes would captivate, hypnotize, paralyze you. I could have the answer written on the sheet in front of me, yet I could not tear my eyes from her glare to glance down.

My parents spoke French at home. We had learned many phrases growing up. When we wanted to converse without others being aware for family privacy, we would slip over into French. Money, purchases, family matters, illness, dinner, choices out, and friends were often described with words from that language. Despite that background, I struggled in the class. Sister Claire *always* wanted to meet with my mother.

In between those two classrooms, math and French, one year my mother met the bouncing young gentleman in charge of music. I cannot sing. I don't know an "A" from a "B" in music, let alone a sharp from a flat. What I lacked in knowledge and musical aptitude, I attempted to make up for in volume. Mom was an accomplished musician with a beautiful voice. I'm sure my screams of verse after verse grated on Mom's nerves. For graduation, music was required. We both prayed it would not bring my overall grade down too much. To help my music grade, I had written a paper about opera. The Instructor was enthralled with my "interest and understanding of music."

He didn't realize that I loathed my piano lessons. I prayed the teacher would die or any other excuse to not have him come that particular week. I struggled along on the ivory keyboard of my mother's baby grand piano for years. Finally, I cajoled my way into getting a guitar instead. Without piano lessons, I managed finally to worm my way out of guitar too. It "hurt my fingers" and took time from my studies.

When the music teacher asked my mother, on the stairs, if I was planning "to make a career of music" and he hoped "that she would allow me to consider it," I thought she would fall down the entire flight.

Rarely at a loss for words, Mom only stammered out that I would be "heading for college."

Sister Mary Schmidt lived and breathed science. For Mom, her room was always a pleasant, quick visit. A wild woman in her younger days, she had worked in a missionary in Mexico or Central America and learned to drive a stick shift and repair the damage she had done to the vehicle in doing so. She taught us not to believe in spontaneous generation. That mice did not spontaneously spring from boxes of rags, just because you could end up seeing them there if some grain were spread around, just as flies did not spontaneously generate from honey spilled in the kitchen. She was always challenging, asking, inquiring, and loved to learn.

Mr. Ramish taught English. What bit of correct grammar and writing I learned was founded squarely in his class and a little booklet of rules that he printed, published, and shared. He was also the drama instructor. I was known for my ability to acquire the materials we needed for our productions, like handcuffs from the local police, borrowed for the prison scene in "Les Misérables."

Each of those High School individuals gave breadth and substance to the knowledge I would use to skyrocket through college. I was in shock, though, for my first college English paper to get a "D," as in "David," as in "dog," as in "die." I went to the professor personally, having learned from those parent/teacher conferences, and Dad's debate training and political campaigns that you needed to go after what you wanted, aggressively, articulately. The Professor explained he wanted to get my attention because I could do so much more than I had on that particular piece. He would expect never to see such a simple attempt on my part again. I never had another grade besides "A" from his courses.

College was a whirlwind. It was the revolving door to get me to the other side, medical school. I could have been in an automatic five-year program through Penn State. Once you are accepted, you spend the next five years between their campus and Jefferson Medical School in Philadelphia and come out a physician by the age of 22 or 23. (You needed to be placed high enough in your graduating class and score high enough on your SAT. I had scored high enough on the PSAT, but on the SAT, I just missed the cut-off. The average score for Pennsylvania was hundreds less and I was damned if I was going to retake the test, just to qualify to go to some enormous university to be a nameless number, ground up like so much fodder— but that didn't mean I planned to take anymore time transitioning to medical school.)

Starting in the fall of 1978, I proceeded to take all four years of college classes for a biology-based four-year degree in less than two years. By the spring of 1980, I had all but eight credits to graduate. I was hell-bent for leather—an odd saying, describing perhaps the early horse and riders delivering the mail hunched over the saddle, horse's reins in each hand, whipping their steeds to a lather, heading to the next stop and safety, looking neither right nor left. I was driven in just such a fashion, frantic not to be derailed from the path that I had set by any distraction or danger. It seemed everything I did in those days focused around the fastest, surest path to becoming a modern medical woman.

It was important to have excellent grades to be considered for medical school, but more important to have the most outstanding of those grades in math and science.

Medical schools looked at the average grades of math and science separately from those, "skipping through the tulips, basket weaving I and II" courses that they considered "the arts" to be. I made every effort to have the very best Grade Point Average, or GPA, in science, as math, calculus, was very difficult. I certainly prayed my way through college-level calculus. The poor man who taught my second year of that course got a tumor of the eye and had to leave the course for surgery. It was a miracle that he survived. His farewell to the class was A's for all of us in that semester, a gift to be sure and much appreciated.

Harder to acquire, were the six credits of science, A's that I managed to get in the month of May. Spring break time, I spent on a break from normal academics by living in the Allegheny National Forest, with two of our biology professors. They had a grant to study the local flora and fauna. If you wrote out your papers clearly enough for them to turn it in as their own research, it seemed to all but assured, an A for those six Ecology credits that you earned. We slept on the ground, washed up in cold water, ate at the campfire, and trapped bats in nets over creeks at dusk. We live-trapped small mammals through the night, and rescued them to catalogue them before dawn, when the chill in the trap would do them harm. I had to get a fishing license to be able to capture and catalogue salamanders. I studied all manner of plants. We counted every item on the allotted patches of ground, from the trees to the individual blades of grass. I learned to differentiate types of trees by their bark or leaf. We determined their age, as well as their tolerance to shade, water and soil conditions. All things that would be useful at different times later in life, but for the moment, were merely an avenue to acquire a grade. The key to a slot in a medical school class.

Unfortunately, on that trip, I got sick as a dog, as I was living like one on the ground in a tent. One of my college roommates, Judy, took me to a little community Emergency Room near her hometown of Kane, PA. Fever, swollen throat, delirious. Attired in jeans and flannel shirt, with a Bowie knife strapped to my hip, I declined to get completely undressed for the Emergency Room clinician who wanted to examine me. I pointed silently to my throat through my open mouth. I couldn't talk well from the swelling and pain there. I gripped the handle of my Bowie knife with my other hand. I must have been a sight to behold. I don't think he even listened to my chest through my flannel shirt. He declared it was not Diphtheria and that I would survive. Just as important, I got my A for six science credits!

I was an arrogant, awful, immature individual, demanding, defiant, and working on becoming a force to be reckoned with. My summer of college, I took dozens of credits and researched how I could get in as many of those "artsy" classes as required. Gannon did not let you get away with just math and science. You would be well-rounded if you graduated from there. They required Theology, Sociology, and Philosophy, as well as Literature and Art. We actually had a School of Drama there and while I appreciated viewing their productions, I did not participate; I was a little busy taking lots of classes.

That summer was no exception. There was a group going from the United States over to Spain to study. The professors were from our country so that the courses would be given in English. We would get *American* credits. I would be able to take Language, English, Sociology, Theology and Philosophy. Because of the timing, I would have *fewer* days in school than if I had stayed in Erie. It would include room and board and a chance to do some limited travel in Europe and would cost less money than summer school at Gannon. This did not take a math major to figure out; Europe would be the better plan. I met with the professors to see if I could work with them. I talked with students who had done the courses so I would be sure that I could accomplish the straight A's I needed for medical school acceptance. Plans were made.

I spoke not a word of Spanish. Luckily, Judy, also interested in medicine, my companion from the forest excursion, would be going, too. She spoke fluent Spanish. I had found that college was a much better place to study French. In my summer before going into Gannon, at the community college, I improved the basics that my family had started. I believed I could adapt. Someone told me, "Just speak French slowly enough, and wear a short enough skirt." The languages were fairly close; I was sure that by sticking close to Judy, I could manage. With that philosophy, the first words I had to learn in Spanish were, "leave me *alone!*"

Medical schools wanted to see that you had some interest in your community, that you were a well-rounded individual. I carefully selected my extracurricular activities for the same path as my academics. I joined a service fraternity instead of a sorority and volunteered with the Red Cross. I participated in a Survivalist Outdoors Club, including rafting down the Yough River (never mind I couldn't swim), camping out in the winter months in New York and Erie, and other crazy stunts designed to prove that I could survive anything.

With my carefully collected academic credits and extracurricular notations, I was ready to select a medical school. My friend and counselor of years' past, Ed Bash, had helped me find a Pennsylvania medical school called Hahnemann in Philadelphia. Originally known for its holistic approach to medicine, it had blossomed into Cardiology, Neurology, Cancer research, and most recently, was renowned for its graduates in the new field of *Family*

Practice. I was on my way. Several early roommates from Gannon had fallen by the wayside and dropped out of the Pre-Med and Science program. By the end of twenty months, when I had accumulated nearly all of my four years' worth of credits, there were only six of us who were offered interviews, from the original sixty-three who had proudly started on this program together.

I took our enormous, red Lincoln Towne Car, tank of a family vehicle, and drove across the state. In my slip, so as not to wrinkle the outfit I would be wearing for my interview. I sped to face the Evaluation Committee at Hahnemann in the wood-paneled, leather-chaired boardroom. I pulled into the parking lot, got out of the vehicle, put on my suit over my slip, and strode for the first time through the doors where I would spend my next four years. There was no such guarantee, you understand, but *I knew.* There were others there that day for interviews. In retrospect, I barely have a recollection of other candidates as shaky, nervous, wisps along the walls in the interim where I waited for my interview's assigned time. I had accumulated not only a collection of academic achievements, honors and awards for community activities, but quite an attitude to go with them. When my name was called, L.H. Fuge strode decisively through the doors of the Boardroom. I acknowledged our cursory introductions.

At the first harsh, demanding, and seemingly demeaning question of, "And why should we accept you?" I tossed my portfolio with my application across their desk like skipping a stone across a lake.

I stood to the maximum of my significant height, tossed my head back and declared, "Because if you don't accept me, on this early acceptance now, my application will *not* cross your desk again and it will be your loss!" I turned on my heel and left the interview. Some angel must have intervened, for the rest is history.

LHF studies small cellular components of human tissue

CHAPTER NINETEEN
Second Chances

Immature and arrogant and, in retrospect, inadequately prepared academically, I arrived at medical school, a mere twenty years old. I had worked in the family's Law office, done checks and banking for the home since the age of nine, spent seemingly every waking minute dreaming for this day since the age of thirteen. I was in no way prepared for the harsh reality of competing either with the top one percent of students from schools around the country, who had fought their way to this opportunity, or the instructors, who had no personal interest in our surviving their classes. The school had been paid their twenty-thousand-dollar tuition for the year. There were literally hundreds of alternative candidates clamoring for the opportunity to take our places. There were no refunds.

There were many students who left the program. I, too, flunked out of medical school. Saying it now, it seems so odd. Having been a practicing physician for more than twenty years, accomplished in teaching, administration, and clinical care, I see how that harsh first year of medical school forever changed the person who entered it. I swear "there should be no atheists in fox holes or medical schools." Each day, each course was a battle for me. I was fortunate to have a family who expected that I would succeed and the personal drive to overcome adversity. I left medical school a different person than I entered: humble, appreciative, and a better doctor than I ever could have been otherwise.

There were many factors that made that first year in medical school difficult, not the least of which was that all my other classmates had had two more years of education than I did. I had rushed through getting the required minimums for medical school admissions. I did not take college level of any of the classes that I would be taking in medical school, such as histology, microbiology, pathologies, or even the more advanced biochemistries. Every word, every sentence, every book, every nuance was *new* data to be memorized. Medical school professors would start out the day with the assumption that you had read the next six chapters of their text since the previous day. Somehow, you knew it, or you had taken this course in college a year or two ago. They were simply a brief refresher, too bad if you didn't get it. My blessing and curse was the fact that, my education to this point had been easy. I had never had to learn how to study carefully or in-depth, with totally new material that seemed to make no sense whatsoever.

I had not had the privilege of dealing with so many other brilliant individuals before medical school. A great collection of more than two hundred and fifty brilliant, young, eager minds per class. Stiff competition, to be sure.

Then there was the living arrangement. I had spent my months in college traveling back and forth home every weekend. We called two to three times a week for extended conversations. Family wrote scores of letters to encourage me, because I said I wouldn't study any day I didn't get mail. My mother dutifully typed a letter at least every day for the mailman. My grandparents wrote on a weekly basis; even my sister and aunt corresponded at times. With frequent trips back and forth, my photo album of memories to review and letters prodding me on, I had managed not to be too homesick. Philadelphia was more than six hours across the state from home, with no transportation or time available to travel. Philadelphia seemed to have no greenery or even sunshine. I would walk from my little ten-and-one-half by twenty-foot room across the expressway to my classroom, sometimes too despondent and distracted even to look for traffic. Many classmates were in the same boat; dozens of us would wander across the ten to twelve lanes of traffic at the start or end of each day. Miraculously, no one was killed. God must have been watching over us all.

That year, my father's politically-appointed court position was abruptly terminated after eighteen and a half years. It was a huge part of our family income and he was only months from retiring. It was a year when "pride" no longer propelled me. I opted to go through the process of appeals, which apparently, were rarely asked for and never won. I prayed they would reconsider my termination from school. No pride, just determination. I not only requested my right to appeal, but demanded to do it *in person*. The school's written rule book says that was a possibility, but face-to-face had never been asked for, nor agreed to before. I hoped that by going in person the individuals on the appeals board might see me as an individual for the first time. If they got to look into my eyes, hear the extenuating circumstances of this last year from my lips, and see the passion for healing in my heart, perhaps they would look into their hearts and recommend my reinstatement to medical school.

There was a group of twenty professors and administrators in that room. A more terrifying room I've never entered. At best, my audience was disinterested, some even turned away from me and put the backs of their chairs towards me as I spoke. They were required to be there. They were not required to care. My arch nemesis, the head of biochemistry, Dr. Baghdad, orchestrated the proceedings of that day and introduced me to that room. I presented my impassioned plea clearly and articulately, like a superbly choreographed political campaign or classic debate argument, with synopsis of reasoning, individual points of fact, and a conclusion they should agree with. I spoke with emotion from the heart, without even glancing at the note cards in front of me. I need not have rehearsed this presentation hundreds of times. I had lived it. No written reminders were needed to share it, even with this daunting group of onlookers. Perhaps I had persuaded some. Most were listening to me by the conclusion of the allotted minutes I had been allowed to state my case.

Baghdad, I'm not sure if that was exactly his name, was the head of biochemistry. Perhaps that name sticks in my mind now more because of the difficulties in the Middle East. Regardless, he escorted me from the room, closed the door, and curtly explained that I would receive an acknowledgement of the committee's decision. I left and went home.

I took his call when it came. My appeal had been denied. I was calm and thinking clearly. I asked, "What is the next step of the appeal process?" He faltered. Apparently there was a next step, although it had not been taken, maybe ever. And to hear me request it calmly, dispassionately and matter-of-factly, as my only response to his seemingly grim news, seemed to surprise him. The Board of Trustees would name a group of three to a subcommittee to review my materials. I thanked him for his call. I would be taking that next step of appeal. My materials for it would be delivered to him and the Board shortly.

The angels were with me. The Board of Trustees of that exalted institution named Director Peter Amenta, head of all of the Anatomies of their renowned institution and my mentor for histology, to head the group of three that would re-review my case. Miraculously, my petition was accepted. I would be allowed to re-do the first year of medical school. I was back on the path of my dream. I went to tell my parents and figure out where I would find another $25,000 to borrow to do this again, differently, better. I was certainly a different individual who entered those doors to restart my first year of medical school.

Histology is the study of small stuff, the cells that make up each type of our body's tissues. I spent my time there, looking through a microscope and studying the book Dr. Amenta wrote, internationally naming each anatomy item in nomenclature that could be understood by clinicians from all countries.

"Don't sweat the small stuff," was something I learned from him. I learned that everything *is* small stuff. The life's lesson he gave me, emphasizes how crucially important second chances are. I think of him to this day. I called him every time I made an additional step forward in my dream, even years after I graduated from medical school. I still took less than the usual time to accomplish my extensive education, seven years, instead of the normal eight. It could have been six, but without him, it wouldn't have been at all. He applauded when I became Assistant Chief Resident, when I made Chief Resident, when I was became Chairman

LHF MD LOVE, HUMOR, FAITH: MY DESTINY

of the Department of Family Practice, and when I was elected President of the entire medical staff. I think he'd be proudest of the care I've given to every patient and the positive, kind attitude I've tried to have every day, because I learned them from him.

LHF as Chief Resident of Family Practice, in her office

Pap-pap with Nana on their 50ᵗʰ Anniversary (left)

***Grandpap with Grandma Nancy
on their 50th Anniversary (right)**

CHAPTER TWENTY
Over My Dead Body

Nana and Pap-pap were very affectionate people. Growing up, we kids did not get to see them often. When we did, it was common to see Pap-pap grab Nana as she walked by. He would pull her into his lap, hold her and kiss her or wrap his arms around her as he walked by, pat her on the bottom, ("po-po" as we kids called it), and shower her with kisses. There was no shortage of physical love and affection in their household.

This was a stark contrast to my father's parents, whom we saw all the time. They were never mean with each other. There was no screaming or swearing, but they were stern, quiet people who had to be encouraged to stand beside each other for a photo. Ray and Nancy Fuge did not show outward affection. Rarely smiling, never touching, they were respectful with each other, just short of distant. If there were two pieces of furniture in the room, they would not sit beside each other, even on the couch. For a person coming from that upbringing, it is natural that my father would call Mom to come to the hallway or the next room to kiss her goodbye rather than do so in front of us children. Mom, however, taught us kids to hug and give kisses, to touch and to say the words of affection that she had grown up with. As neither of the folks had any vision, it was never considered acceptable to run in the door, nod or wave, and run up the stairs. You had to touch and speak, to say hello.

Grandpap Fuge firmly ruled the household, though Grandma Nancy was a formidable woman. She was no slip of a girl like Nana, who had been only a teen when she was whisked away from a life of service in other people's homes to be the darling of Pap-pap's life. Pap-pap showered Nana with affection, if not riches.

Grandma Nancy (Fuge) had been one of nearly a dozen children. As one of the oldest, she was a slave to the family, even left to sleep on the porch at night, when she had caused some small infraction. Growing up, I suspect she had learned to guard her feelings well. She had learned to follow the rules to get along. One of Grandpap's rules was that she was not to cut her hair. He liked her long hair. We rarely saw it down.

She braided my long hair and taught me how to form a quick crown of it up on top of my head, out of the way for patient care. I got so good at doing it; I would do that in the car while driving to the hospital for my surgical training at five-something in the morning.

LHF in crown of braids

Grandma Nancy used little jewelry, perhaps at Grandpap's direction. When Grandpap passed away, Grandma Nancy cut her hair and got her ears pierced. I can almost see her standing over his open coffin with its beautiful blue satin-rose design lining, with her special new hair-do and earrings, a soft smile on her lips. As an adult, I can insert words to go with her smile. He had laid down the law that, "you will cut your hair over my dead body" and so, it seemed, she did!

Grandma Nancy with her new hairdo and pierced earrings*

LHF hanging out at the bar on the cruise ship for food and ice

CHAPTER TWENTY-ONE
Fiasco Cruise

My Kid sister is only three years younger than I. Despite the near fourteen years we spent living under the same roof, I could not say that, we were friends growing up. At times, we were not even friendly. It seemed that Mom purposely kept us at odds with each other, maybe so we would not gang up on her. Regardless of why, we fought. I had the size advantage. Kid had the sharp nails. Many were the time I would hold her away from me at arm's length by the wrists to keep her daggers from causing severe injury. Mom was sure I would break her wrist some day.

Despite our differences, we did try to communicate with each other. Our parents' hearing was so excellent, we were sure that they could hear our conversations three floors away. The old ventilation duct system of the house may have had something to do with it. Still, near them a whisper was certain to be overheard. To overcome their advantage, we went so far as to learn the alphabet in sign language.

Kid hated school. I could not have loved it more. I had an easier time with school work. I was close to Dad. She was inseparable from Mom. Often I would drag her down the sidewalk the short distance from home to elementary school. Dissimilar and occasionally hostile, surprisingly, Kid was still there for me when I needed her.

The previous Mayor, Justice of the Peace and others from our town had gone to jail when Dad took over the Police force as Mayor himself. Dad had taught me how to throw a punch. Trained in wrestling and martial arts, he wanted his daughter to be able to defend herself. "Knee to groin, heel to arch of foot, heel of hand to bridge of nose or gouge the eyes; do whatever you need to stay safe," Dad instructed. When a local teen slapped my braces-filled mouth, it was Kid who sprang into action. The guy looked like he had tangled with a mountain lion defending her cub.

I left for college and Medicine and Kid left home and High School a year early. Kid started with Community College and a lab certificate. She went on to work nights at the coroners' lab while earning her Bachelor of Science and Teaching degrees. Constantly trying new things, she kept busy in the six years we were apart. Antique co-op, Jewelry "store," original stained glass productions, oil painting, old house refurbishing and breeding Samoyed dogs were just a few of her enterprises.

For Kid's college graduation, the folks decided to congratulate her with a cruise to the islands. I had already finished both college and Medical school without much ado, but they did say that I could go too. My invitation seemed like an afterthought or chaperone duty, but free is free. We had both gone to Mom's school of packing *lots*, so our luggage was extensive for the one-week excursion. Arm in arm, with the airport valet trailing behind with the bags, we were off on our grand adventure.

Years before, in school, we had traveled to Canada with the Junior High French class. That was a disappointment. No one to carry the bags, cold weather, limited funds for any side trips from the tiny, dirty motel with six to eight crammed in a room. This would be different: our own cabin on board a well-known cruise line to the warm Bahamas from Miami. Adults now, we took our own money, just in case.

The airport layovers were not ideal, but we sat on the floor and speculated about our big welcome to Miami. Mom had always wanted to go to Hawaii. For their anniversary, Dad took all of us the year I was eleven. The welcome committee had showered us with flowers and hugs while we waited in the shade for the transport to take us directly to our lavish hotel. How much better would this be? We wondered.

Miami was not Hawaii. We had to walk all the way out to the ship. We stood in long lines in the heat, eventually shoved along like cattle into ever-more-narrow paths to climb the steep ramp to the deck. Finally, an official from the cruise line unceremoniously spun us around and someone snapped our picture. "That will be five dollars for the photo," and "Don't worry. We'll get a better one of you next time." What do you mean, next time? We thought.

The "cabin" was minuscule, just enough space for two bunk beds with a narrow path next to them. The bathroom was in a little tiled area at the foot of the beds, with a shower head over the toilet seat. There was one tiny cupboard with a mirror, hardly enough to store one of our sets of travel outfits. There was a noisy room across the hall with electrical outlets, for all those on our deck level to share, for curling irons, contact cleaning kits, etc. Oh well, we would not be spending much time inside anyway.

The first port of call was Mexico. "This is not the Love Boat. Be back on time or we will leave without you," we were warned. Transport to shore had not been included in our package. "That would be extra." Kid did not want to spend her money yet, so I paid for us to get to shore for the bus tour of the local ruins. The bus had no air-conditioning, but no glass in the windows either. Warm pop was available for only three dollars. The swarm of insects that attacked Kid was the really bad part. She swelled up like a puffer fish. Waiting for the ferry back to the cruise liner, I tried to cool Kid's fever down by renting snorkels. The cool water should have helped, but she got cut on the coral instead.

At the second port of call, Kid would not get off the ship. She didn't care who paid. I went ashore and she stretched out on deck. By my return, she was redder than a fresh boiled lobster from head to toe. She could not even get sandals on her feet. Ice was in short supply; we could buy mixed drinks from the bar and get a few pieces. I decided to use the stronger air conditioner in the movie theater, in addition to Tylenol, to cool Kid off. We took the sheet off the bunk, wet it down in the "shower" and wrapped her in it.

Food was limited. If you did not make it to the assigned times for the dining room, you could go hungry. The lavish displays of tropically-decorated tables seen in brochures were not evident until we returned to port at Miami. They were a photo op—not for consumption. Meal times were assigned in advance of the trip: "early" or "late." If you wanted to get dinner before nine o'clock, you had to take breakfast at six o'clock. Getting up that early did not work out. The first day, we missed eating. Then we found out about "room service." There was no selection, just a note you could leave on your doorknob by midnight, with the number of people who would be in your cabin for breakfast. The next day we listed the two of us. We did get food, albeit at dawn: three ounces of orange juice, a half slice of bacon and a half a piece of toast each!

A skewer of fresh fruit could be obtained in the bar in some of the tropical drinks. Dress appealingly and someone might even buy it for you: low-cut top, tight waist, short skirt, bra optional. The following night, our note said there would be six of us for breakfast in our cabin. They probably thought we were having an all night orgy; we got a better quantity of breakfast delivered.

Unfortunately, we hit rough seas. Kid got very seasick. Meals did not matter so much after that. By our last port of call, Jamaica, Kid paid to get off the ship. We were told, "Don't drink the water." Still a little queasy, she just sucked on the ice. On our return voyage, when she was not on our little toilet, Kid was writhing back and forth on the bottom bunk, holding her belly. My last remaining remedy with us was a bottle of codeine cough medicine. I gave it to her and instructed, "Drink until I tell you to stop." Doped to sleep for the remainder of the adventure, Kid had managed to lose eleven pounds on a one-week cruise.

Neither of us has considered another sea voyage, free or not, but the fiasco trip started our bonding as friends for our adult life.

LaDonna in gown and veil

CHAPTER TWENTY-TWO
Praying for Strength

I was married first when I was very young—maybe immature is a better word. It was a storybook wedding . . . beautiful, spectacular, memorable in every way. Many, many, people showed extra consideration and caring for me by making that day possible and full of beautiful memories. While it was a Cinderella wedding, it was a nightmare marriage. I was fortunate to get out alive. There were lots of difficulties leading up to that first wedding day, foreshadowing that could have cautioned against trouble ahead. My failures to heed these warnings led me to that beautiful wedding day and the difficult life that followed.

Mac and I had known each other since I was thirteen. Back then, he was a single father with a very young boy, a lovely, wonderful, bright, quiet, pleasant child. I was infatuated. I would have done anything to please. Fortunately, there was not time for sex. I'm not sure I'd have had the good sense to keep myself safe.

Mac had been my swim coach at the local high school. He taught swimming and diving. He was quite adept and had certificates in deep sea diving. I had grown up with a mother who didn't like swimming. I can recall having only inches of water in the bathtub. On my first trip to the local city pool—I would have been ten or twelve—I had no clue about how to swim. That's how I ended up back at the high school gym for swimming lessons. This instructor's concept was to have you make trip after trip after trip up onto the diving board and dive into the water. Once you're in, you figure out how to get to the side so you don't drown. What was *not* included was how to dive in a way that would be safe. So, time after time, get up, get the gumption to jump off and smack, like a pancake, face down, spread eagle in the water. It didn't take long for me to be red as sunburn. Jump after jump after smack after slam after try. I don't remember now if the lessons were half an hour or an hour. That did not matter, I was trying to please.

Over the years, when Mac had moved out of the area, we wrote back and forth, affectionate pen pals. He had poor handwriting with bad grammar and worse spelling. He was the older man; I was the infatuated child, no matter how many years had passed.

As an adult, I flew down to that area of the country. I was doing a national presentation on research I had done. We met again. It was magical, romantic. He wined and dined me, and took me dancing. Dancing, by the way, is a dangerous thing. Mac would hold me in his arms, spin me around and take my breath away. I was flying. I was not thinking straight. Dancing is definitely something to be careful of. When he asked me to marry him, I said yes.

His church was in Louisiana. I did not have one that would work for a wedding. We went looking for a local option. Monroeville, Pennsylvania had a beautiful, historic church, all made out of local fieldstone, with spectacular stained glass windows. A local group used "The Old Stone Church" for their services. It seemed the perfect spot. On one of Mac's trips in this direction, we met with the minister for the little local congregation. He seemed to be a very reasonable person. He talked to us about spiritual bonding and how he ran his wedding services. He tried to have a few planning meetings with the couple. It all seemed to go fairly well.

On my trip down to Louisiana, where Mac and I had met up again, I was doing a research presentation called "Visual Birth Debriefing." My research included taking photographs when new moms gave birth. I delivered their babies, and then took a picture of mother and child. Later, we used these photographs to talk about all the good and bad aspects of the deliveries—what they would change. It gave them an opportunity to work out anything that was bothering them. Plus, they got a picture with their babies. I found photographs to be therapeutic.

I did not have photographs growing up. It was not something we did. I teased that I was the walking, talking, Seeing Eye dog, being the firstborn child of my blind folks. This description was not quite accurate, as they were highly competent and ambulatory on their own, but an explanation for how close our bond was. Our extreme closeness made it difficult for me to be away, even for a short period, so I got a Polaroid camera and took pictures of everybody! Our garden, each room of the house, mom in her kitchen, dad at his desk, the list went on and on. Before I left for college, I'd made an entire photo album to take with me. When I was homesick, or struggling, I would look through that book. It's a miracle the pages didn't fall out in that first year, as often as I went through it. Between that first time away from home at college until doing research as a young physician, pictures had become a crucial part of how I handled life, the good and the bad. Of course my wedding must have pictures.

At the close of the third visit, the Reverend told us one

last rule: There would be no photos during the wedding. That point was not negotiable. He was right. It wasn't. We needed a new minister. Obstacle one.

The date was rapidly approaching. Only four months before the wedding date, we found a local Justice of the Peace, a Doctor of English, who could perform our service. Our date, that we had for the church was *his* wedding anniversary. Obstacle Two. He asked his wife. She graciously agreed for him to marry this young couple on their anniversary, before he came home and celebrated with her. Thank you. We were set. The Doctor *would* do our service at the beautiful stone church.

The next situation: my sister. *She* wanted purple for the bridesmaids. You would have thought it was her wedding, for as many details as she filled in. The dresses she helped pick were lovely. To cut costs, I actually sewed the matching headpieces for her and my college and medical school roommates: beautiful little teardrop-shaped miniature hats with lace and flowers to complement the dresses. I sewed on decorative flowers, and made the altar cloth by hand. I always sewed much better by hand than by machine. I worked on them in any spare minutes for weeks.

Obstacle Three: our Doctor was walking across the street and got run over. He was in the intensive care unit the week before our service! I was frantic. One of the physicians at the hospital graciously introduced her minister, part of a nondenominational church I'd never heard of. He was willing.

We planned a rehearsal of church set-up, reading the poems we had written, and figuring out where to stand and walk. The church had no center aisle — a little different. We figured we'd manage just fine, if we got folks together to practice. And what happened? Obstacle Four: The minister got lost on the way to rehearsal. He never got there!

I was living at least twenty minutes away from my hospital, more from the stone church. Kid had been "flipping" real estate, buying cheap, fixing up quick, and selling for a profit. I had bought one with a down payment to her plus a loan from my folks – complete with interest. The night before the wedding, I was staying in my little home. My college roommate, Judy, and a medical classmate, Jan, both arrived there safely. What happened? The furnace at the house quit. Obstacle Five. Now, since this happened to be January; it was a little bit of a problem. We didn't have any hot water. We didn't have any heat. We all huddled together. I can remember having to do my nails with my fingers poking out through the holes of an afghan, huddling up to try and stay warm. Was it a warning?

The plan had been to congregate at a little local hotel in Monroeville before the wedding, to dress, as there was not much space to primp and fuss in The Stone Church. People, gown and veil would meet up in a pre-paid suite of rooms. (One of the other ladies from work, a nurse by the name of Miss Joan, had made the veil for me from an enormous, beautiful piece of lace and little petite flowers.) The hotel was just a block from the stone church and it had parking, which the stone church did not. We hurried and scurried in flannel shirts, to find a place to wash and set my hair with no notice. Then we were off to the little local fire hall, decorations in tow. Many of the young doctors and their wives showed up to help set up. Only then were we told that nothing could be taped or tacked up on the walls or ceilings. "Oops," or something more like my Mimi would say, "Like to make a body swear!" A nearby flower shop sold helium-filled balloons. I bought dozens. They lifted our decorations towards heaven.

That minor problem solved, we proceeded to roll out the yards of streamers, only to find that no one had scissors.

There was nothing to cut the streamers and strings to finish the decorations. Not to be deterred, I went out to my car and brought in a Bowie knife, like something from the Daniel Boone movies, maybe a foot long, for these little ladies and doctors to cut crepe paper and satin.

Next, I met everybody congregating in the lobby of the hotel, not in our suites! The disgruntled, concerned, and distressed individual at the front desk explained that there was a women's conference and that they had given away our rooms. This was the morning of the wedding!

The hotel wanted the more than fifty young physicians who came to the hospital each year to still want to stay with them. They tried desperately to make some kind of accommodations for us. After all, I was the hospital's chief resident.

We managed. It all came together. Everyone was dressed beautifully. The colors were just right. Everyone remembered what to say and where to stand. The booklets were there with all the special things that we had written. The family came, both sides, and all the doctors from the hospital where I worked showed up. The dress was beautiful and delicate. The attendants all matched spectacularly. We had the most lovely service and reception.

People asked later, "Weren't you praying about this?" when one after another, after another, after another, problem arose. I sure was praying. I was praying for *strength* instead of *guidance*. In retrospect, I got only what I asked for; I persevered and had a spectacular Cinderella wedding.

In the years after my short and stormy marriage with Mac, I have been asked about him by those who were involved in our lavish nuptials. To avoid opening up my scarred-over wounds from that time in my life, I have found a short way of explaining how I ended up having that marriage annulled: "It may have been a story tale service, but it was a nightmare life."

I was *sure* that I would never get attached to anyone again, let alone remarry, however, Church and friends joined together to introduce me to a protector, with whom I would eventually fall in love.

LHF demonstrates
trimming wedding decorations with a Bowie knife

*Tiny has "lived" on Dr Fuge's stethoscope for 25 years. Koala's have bigger ears & she can show kids the ear exam better on them.

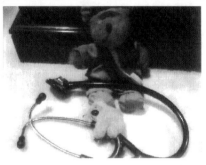

Hunting positives in the compilation of the pieces of her past

LaDonna (LHF) graduated from Hahnemann Medical School with the dark green velvet hood of a doctor. The two LHFs share a rare silly moment. It was an ironic comparison to Lloyd's Honors graduation from Pitt and Law School decades before. With no vision, he has been a tough role model.

LaDonna's Mom went blind from meningitis soon after this picture (top left).

"GRAMMIES" graduation picture (above) from the School for the Blind has an odd resemblance to LHF's picture for starting school (Right).

"GRAMMIES"
(top left) as a
girl,
is seen with *her*
"Nana."

Grammies' Mimi
(top right photo)
is seen with her young
family, including
Grammies' dad
(on the left).
We called him
Pap-pap.

Before, during and
after marrying,
Grammies' parents
were an affectionate
couple (seen here).
We always called
Grammies' Mother
"Nana."

Lloyd's parents (Grandma Nancy and Grandpap– see below) were stoic people as adults.

Above, (left in top left photo) Grandma Nancy enjoyed great, carefree friendships as a young person.

LHF's Grandpap enjoyed going out with his hunting dog in the woods behind their Clairton home (above right).

Fuges are pictured by their home. In the background can be seen a trellis for the flowers he enjoyed so much.

Before he lost his eyesight in an explosion as a teen, Lloyd is seen here with his own dog.

After years of reconstructive surgeries, Lloyd is back home with a new pup (below) before leaving for the School for the Blind to start his spectacular academic career of honors, awards and eventually a Law Degree from Pitt.

Married at Heinz Chapel in Pittsburgh PA on the 13th, the Fuge's have enjoyed decades of good luck. Despite both being blind, they were active in philanthropies and politics. (*Seen below hosting their annual *indoor* Christmas carol party.)

*Their 40 by 40 foot living room was the scene for many gala events. It included two fireplaces, a baby grand piano, an organ, and two sets of couches. For thirty years, since LaDonna designed and hand made the above nine-foot long hook rug, it hung in their palatial residence, on continuous display with afghans & other crafts.

446 Mitchell Avenue was home to the Fuge family until spring 2007, but it was first built in the 1930s for the head of the mill.

*It looked much the same when LHF left for her whirlwind medical education. Despite metal siding and trim, the green on white looked comfortingly the same, upon her return.

Mailers went out by the
tens of thousands for the
FUGEs in the many political campaigns for mayor and judge.
(Photo top right, *LHF on right*, Kid on the left.)In 1973, Lloyd
won his election bid for Mayor of Clairton, PA. His parents, wife
and LaDonna (LHF) are pictured below following his January
inauguration. More than thirty years later, Sikira (their
granddaughter) wore the same rainbow colored dress
Grammies' wore to the 1970s event to sing a solo of "Over The
Rainbow" for her junior high play in Plum PA (top left*).

*Hand quilting is another art form LHF enjoys.

Eight years of ballet classes started with a plan to learn to "just stand straight." LHF went on to "dance" everywhere she went, such as summer vacation (right) in the Laurel Mountains. Later, permutations of fifth position could still be seen as she strode into hospital Board meetings.

Dr. Peter Amenta, head of all the Anatomy Departments at Hahnemann Medical School was a great friend and mentor to LaDonna.

By the time she got to the clinical rotation years of her Medical education, LaDonna was excelling again. LHF has since mentored dozens of young doctors and students herself.

(Seen here on her Obstetrical rotation, LHF always did love to wear *green* and the scrub outfits were comfortable besides.)

LHF won the Poster Presentation award at the National Patient Education conference in Kansas City in 1988 for her work with Obstetrics. Seen here she instructs other clinicians in the process.

Dr. Gloria Kasey, seen here with Dr. LaDonna Fuge on a trip down south, was a friend & colleague.

When Kasey died young from breast cancer, Forbes Foundation created a fund in her name to educate other clinicians on creating the kind of spiritually positive outlook in health care that Dr. Gloria Kasey embodied.

As a young doctor, LHF was required to wear a white coat. She stopped that as soon as protocol would allow, for a softer, friendlier garb. Seen above with her typical koala bears, Dr. Fuge is exhausted after her first all night call.

Years later (below,) she accepts the Golden Apple award for being the best teacher of Residents out of the >800 Attending Physicians on the Forbes Medical Staff. LHF served there as Chairman of Family Practice, President of the Medical Staff and Medical Director.

LHF, Lynne, Meredith, Sr. Carole, Kathy, Nancy, Mary, Dr. Jana and Rachel (left to right), in the public press release of West Penn Allegheny Health System as the innovative practice of 2007.

Below: The CARE Team was this small group of veteran health care staff, lead by Dr. Fuge and her dream of a combined location for exemplary, caring, quality care where *any* good idea could be tried.

LHF, Kathy, Sandy, Lee and Mary left the security of their tenured positions at three different locations to come together to form The first CARE Team. This bottom photo was sent out by the thousands to local zip codes, in 1998, to advise of the group's bold move.

(Sadly, Lee lost her four year fight to ovarian cancer.)

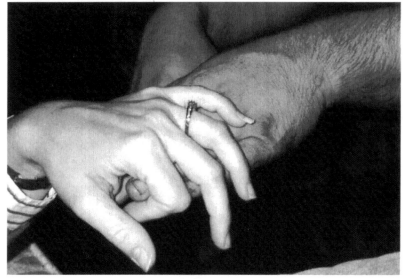

*Despite a difficult time in the past, LHF got engaged to her "cowboy bodyguard" Tom, and the rest, as they say, is history. Below, they share a "Happy New Year's" kiss.

*Tom loved to ride on their little 40 acres of heaven: Promises Kept Farm. Seen below, *Tom walks out on a limb of the massive tree that crushed the house.

LHF and Tom to raised Akitas and American Quarter Horses at Promises Kept Farm, Inc. starting in 1991.

*Spring at the farm seen to the right. For Sikira's 10th birthday, they visited Disney and swam with Dolphin, Jennie. Children were added to the happy family (right).

LHF & Sikira's Disney
Hawaiian
dinner on vacation from the
farm.*

*Promises Kept Farm

Young Wonder - Lloydthomas finds a baby bird*

LHF as girl in frills.
*Sikira plays Doctor

*Horses play as
Spring turns to
*Summer.

*Fall at
Promises Kept Farm.

Sunset at Promises Kept*

New brother arrives.

LHF plays nurse

Africa

THABAZIMBI

New parents accompany infant Sikira to surgeries to try to salvage her deteriorating vision. Seen below on steps of Croatian Orphanage.

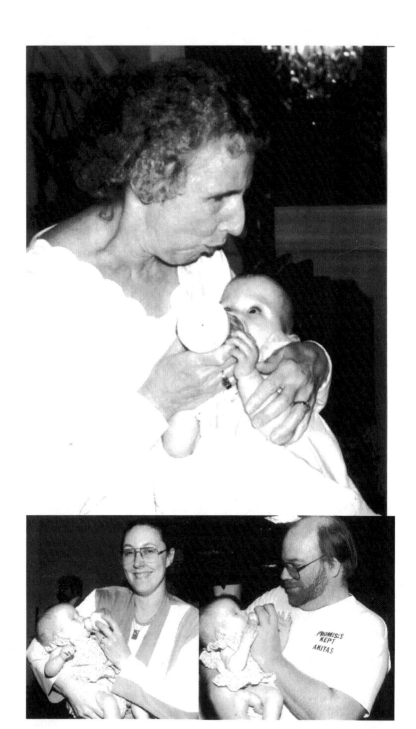

*Sikira watches Grammies, and *enjoys teething on LHF's pewter necklace. *She stands for the first time to be nearer to Tom when he is hospitalized, and sees better for a time in *big* glasses.

*Below, Grandma Nancy holds Sikira, who wears Grandma Nancy's baby ring!

*Sikira's survival in her young years was celebrated with lavish birthday parties. *Sikira wore almost as many frilly dresses as LHF. *Left, Sikira climbs on the back of her protector, the Akita stud, Kodiak. Right, she gets to handle wild birds through the Raptor Rescue Program.

LHF, after four infertility specialists and two adopted children, finally, miraculously, got pregnant. LHF, seen here in July 1999, pregnant and holding son, LT. (Tierra Jean unfortunately miscarried on October 11, 1999.)

LaDonna is seen here washing in the Holy water at the spring in Lourdes, France.

One Christmas, LHF had *nothing* ready. She went on a twelve hour truck ride, with Grammies, the children, the dog, toys, snacks, and music. Despite a snow blizzard day, they got *all* gifts, paper & tree.

For the holiday party of 2006, LT was Mom's date for dinner. After Tom's diet and exercise program, LHF again fit into her green-lace-backless gown from the Fuge's Annual Carol Party of 1989!

*Seen above, LT acts as a young guide for his big sister, Sikira.

*Sikira, learns through great teachers, aides and personal fortitude to walk with a cane and even *run* alone! (*Top left, she is seen running to a softball base that "beeps" in a game of Beep Baseball with local Lion's Clubs.)

*Oreo Innocence at bedtime

*A young LT loves exercise and his local sports team.

Singing lessons to her brother pay off as they develop Sikira's awesome voice. Now having received her own private voice lessons, Sikira's perfect pitch and outstanding range, up to high "C," are a joy at her recitals and chorus performances.

LHF and Sikira get to meet Country singer Brad Pasley at his tour bus. Sikira compliments him on his singing. Sikira especially loves his song about a couple buried under a willow tree. Above, Sikira gives him a photo of her feeling the first willow tree she ever "saw."

Below, Sikira sits on the floor with singer Shania Twain & gives her roses.

*Sikira meets with Martina McBride & discusses fashion. Sikira's rosebud shirt may not have sequins, but it feels just as good as Martina's big letter "M." Sikira loves to sing McBride's song "In My Daughter's Eyes."

*Brother (Lloydthomas), Mom (LHF) and Dad (Tom) all get to meet the great Country Western singing star.

Alan Jackson, Reba and Terri
Clark were each *very* gracious
at their various
visits with Sikira
and LHF!

*Lloydthomas intently scrutinizes Grammies' loving face. Blind does *not* matter to him, they can "*see*" each other fine! *Below, young admiration has LT mimic Tom. *By 2nd grade LT was winning writing awards.

*Teamwork! Sikira and LT enjoy their seesaw in part of Grammies' *huge* living room. Despite their 5 1/2 years difference in age, they make great playmates.

Despite her lack of eyesight, Sikira is bound to protect her two-year-old brother. "I won't let him out the door!" she assures the family. Doesn't look like she'll let him *breathe* either.

*Seen at left, Sikira stops LT at the bottom of the stairs at the door, on his second birthday. He is heading OUT for a special tractor ride that had been promised for later.

*Sikira had hundreds of books that she could feel, or that made sounds, or had areas that she could scratch to smell. She showed her brother early about how great it was to "*read.*" *Eventually, Sikira learns to read Braille with the help of her grandparents (bottom left).

*Sikira uses her fingers to "see" the raised map of Williamsburg Colonial Town (right).

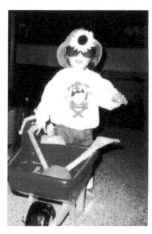

*Sikira always enjoyed gardening. *Left, she touches a weeping willow.

*Brother, LT explains to Sikira, that she does *not* need help to ride *his* two-wheeled bike, because it still has training wheels and he can tell her where to steer.

*LT learns to watch wild life at the farm with Dad. *Above, he says farewell to a friend. One of the brood mares has suffered a stroke and can no longer eat or control her legs and will have to be put down by the vet.

"See one; Do one; Teach one!" was the saying that described how Medical Schools and Hospitals used to educate young doctors. The above family photo of LHF helping the children made cupcakes for their father's birthday is the perfect visualization of the concept.

Happy Mom snuggles Lloydthomas in a carrying sling after his court finalization of his adoption is complete, (bottom, left). Bottom, right LaDonna takes Sikira on a bareback horse ride at their farm. She enjoyed feeling their hides, mane, warmth and movement since she was an infant. Then, it was cleaner to be on horseback than on the stable floor, with the manure.

LaDonna and Sikira relax in the winter sun of South Africa during their 2005 family vacation safari there. 80 degrees in July, it was a nippy 40 at night, but no rain and no bugs meant no shots or malaria risk in that area.

Greater Kudu trophy of a lifetime & best tasting native meat according to LHF.

Harvested with one shot through the heart at 110 yards. (LHF's was just a fraction of an inch larger than Tom's.)

LaDonna did not like flying. Still she arranged to take the children up with local pilot and surgeon, Dr. Naman for an aerial tour of Pittsburgh, PA and then their farm. LHF got almost as green as the landscape she photographed.

The family's little summer cottage sits on just fifty *feet* of ground by a local creek. Much less to care for than the farm, but just as much appreciated.

Original oil painting by Kid given to LHF as a gift*

CHAPTER TWENTY-THREE
Awakening

Years ago it began,
When suddenly all I had planned, changed.
    I was in turmoil.
    I grieved.
    I fought.
    I grieved again.
In my confusion, you found me.
Like Water – soft and gentle,
    Ever flowing,
    Your influence surrounded me;
    Almost imperceptible,
    Yet soothing.
Driven – I sought a high place close to heaven,
Safe – from which to see clearly . . . the world,
    The stars,
    The truth.

I sought strength in numbers,
Then peace in solitude,
And finally found myself, after much travel
Perched upon a majestic Mountain peak.

From the regal, barren summit
I watched the stars and prayed
For solace and understanding.

Through it all, your soft words
Helped to ease my pain and clear my mind.
And I came to know,
That Water – though fluid and yielding,
Through its persistence,
Is powerful enough
To break through the obstacles of life.

Insight struck –
Like an electrical charge
Running up my spine:
Lonely is the beauty that is *not* shared.

And so the Mountain and the Water shall join.
One bringing foundation upon which life may flourish,
The other the nourishment to waken the fertile soil.
Separately strong,
As they entwine,
They enhance each other.
Then – Oh, what beauty we all behold.

I wrote this poem about the difficulties I had with
Medical School, when I thought that getting married for the
first time was a positive thing. Mac and I read it together as
part of the Church service at our wedding. Oddly, now,
years later, my poem seems more perfectly to describe the
tumultuous end of that marriage and the Blessing that came
to me in meeting another. Strong, patient and caring Tom
saved me, and together we have forged a beautiful life.

**LHF rests with a newborn foal
at his mother's feet on the floor in their stable**

CHAPTER TWENTY-FOUR
The Perfect Pair

It was our first Christmas together, Tom's and mine. Just that spring, we had put everything we had into getting our farm. It hadn't been an easy year, but we were happy. It came time to think about what to do for my new husband for the Christmas holidays—something special. Spectacular was the goal, but not too expensive. We made a list of each person for whom we wanted to get gifts, trying to figure out perfect things. Little things, by many people's standards, but just the right things, so that the people would know that they were thought a lot about. We had one roll of wrapping paper, on special—one of those really big fat rolls—so everything would be wrapped identically. Christmas meant a lot to us.

Back to something for my Darling. There wasn't a lot of time between work and the new farm. I wasn't even home to go out shopping. Some horse literature magazines helped me track down a great choice. Our horses, mine and his, were coming to the farm. We were planning to raise colts and fillies to sell. Family of all kinds was important to us. When I found beautiful, small, decorative, artistic horse plates, I got one with a mother horse and her baby.

Though only four to five inches across, it would be the perfect thing to get, delicate and special.

The next dilemma . . . where in the world would a guy put a plate? Was it too impractical? You can't eat on it, only look at it. Neither of us ever had anything like commemorative plates before. I hunted and searched for a way to display something special that was just for looking at, finally finding a place that sold beautiful wooden frames. Tom loves wood and these were exquisitely done. With a little black felt background; the plate would fit right in and could hang up on any wall. They had unusual shapes of frames to choose from, not just simple little squares. An octagon with all those special little corners that were precisely cut — Tom could appreciate that. As a former carpenter, he insisted on getting wood to fit just right. A perfectionist himself, he would know that the frame had been something special to make.

I arranged to have them come to work, so Tom wouldn't see them. In a minute that he was checking on something outside, I rushed them into a box and wrapped it. Now here we were, on Christmas, with a couple of little packages for ourselves. He proudly handed me a gift, in the same wrapping paper as everything else we'd wrapped. I smiled and said, "Thank you," handing him his from beside our little tree.

Lifting the lid, I looked inside my box. I shut the top *quickly*. Since we had used all the same paper, I'd opened the wrong package — his package. I felt terrible. I was so upset that I had opened his package. I had worked so hard to get it for him. I hoped I'd gotten it closed before he had seen the little plate. "I'm sorry, sweetheart!" I moved to slide it back across the floor to him. Well, as it turned out, the very box he was opening *was* my gift to Tom! A beautiful, four-to five-inch, mother and baby horse, cradled in that octagon, dark wood frame. We had gotten each other

— the exact *same* gift! He had chosen that exact same plate. He had found the exact same frame. From four different places, we had brought together two exact same Christmas gifts because, it seemed, we thought the exact same way. We had a perfect pair of decorative plates. We were touched. The plates showed our perfect pair of aligned spirits.

I took one of the beautiful horse plates in its frame to work. We hung the other at the house. Years later, when the house was badly damaged in a severe storm, the repair people knocked our precious plate off the wall. It broke, just a tiny chip and crack out of a corner. But out of all the things that we've accumulated over the years, we probably took that damage the hardest. Fortunately, I had the other one at work. We brought home the one that had been undamaged. Hanging on our wall intact again, it made our life whole. It reminds us still of that first Christmas. At my office, I have a wonderful symbol of love and healing beside my desk, one slightly damaged, cherished commemorative. At home, an intact reminder of that perfect pair. The storm is another story.

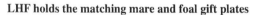

LHF holds the matching mare and foal gift plates

Photo of panorama page in Promises Kept Farm book*

CHAPTER TWENTY-FIVE
The Photographer

Having been raised by two blind parents, photographs were not a big part of my childhood. Still, I created an entire photo album before leaving home for college to act as a therapeutic remembrance, to avoid being too bogged down in homesickness to concentrate on studying and striving for the future. Word got around our extended family that "LaDonna was hunting photographs of her growing-up years." The photo album that I made for college became book number two. Book number one became the collection of photographs taken from various friends, family, and acquaintances over the years of visits, holidays, and gatherings—that included myself, my sister, and my parents. It was an eclectic collection of black and white staged stills and blurry action shots. Some years were missed altogether, except for a wallet-sized school photo to commemorate its passing. Eventually, the collection went on to include occasional photos of my parents as they grew up and then their parents and on back to a more distant and diverse family tree. At the time of this telling, that collection from others is four volumes in size. People had emptied contents of shoeboxes from under beds and out of cupboards and shared small groupings from their ancient, unlabeled collections. I found, sadly, that there was little comment about the people, time, or event that had been captured. I was adamant that this would not happen to me.

Moving forward from college, until I had a family of my own, I photographed everything imaginable, and at times, unimaginable. Painstakingly, I documented the events and thinking and the people in, and behind, each grouping. By the time Tom and I were married, there were some seventy-three photo albums that chronicled the trials and tribulations of the second L.H. Fuge.

I certainly had not become a professional photographer, but I had advanced my way through a number of cameras, "working them to death," my family would say. At first I used small, point and shoot cameras, with drop-in film, acquired from some local store, such as K-Mart, eventually moving to higher-class photography equipment.

I'd learned to appreciate true photographic artwork and unique styles of presentation, like collages of photographs, overlays and panoramas. For my second wedding, I planned a small private church service. Still, I was anxious that Tom and I have someone chronicle our blessed event with photos. I was hoping to find someone with more extensive photographic creativity than I had. I was adamant that this time, marriage would be a lifetime of beauty. I wanted photos to chronicle current blessings and look forward to the joys of tomorrow. I did not know anyone yet who could do that.

The search began by word of mouth, local signage, and thick yellow books of the region. I called more than ninety establishments to find someone who would chronicle our blessed wedding day. Price was last on my list of questions. It didn't seem bizarre to me to think that I might have to finance the photographs for this great day after I got the initial pricing from some of these supposed "artists." What was a surprise was how few had anything to offer but a cookie-cutter approach to a book of a dozen photos. Some even selected staged poses. I asked about doing a collage of photos. "What about doing a vignette, like a photograph of us up in the corner, like the dream or thoughts of a cartoon character in a little bubble?" "Could we have an overlay of two photographs, almost on top of each other to show the people walking up the aisle inside the church, but on top of a photograph of the outside of that architectural structure?" Complicated as these photos may sound in the writing, in my mind's eye, these were simple photographic techniques. Those individuals who had heard of none of them, or would consider none of them, were immediately stricken from the list of consideration.

Soon, I had a very short list to consider. In the end, there were only two under consideration. One was a gentleman from out of the area who would do a photo album of black and white photos that would chronicle your family of origin and the town you grew up in. A novel approach, but he selected the photographs that would be used. The other was a local woman.

Elaine Henigan had no qualms about trying a collage of photographs as I had done with my albums. She had certainly done the overlays and inserts that I spoke of, but had something else to offer: a panorama shot. Elaine would enlarge a picture to twenty-four inches across. That way, it would run over two whole pages of the photo album. What an impressive centerpiece for that beautiful binding of our great day. Thus, Miss Elaine was found, and the Henigan Studios became the photographer for our April 13th wedding.

Our photographer shot a plethora of pictures. Elaine traveled to multiple sites, hiked trails; even lay on the ground for better shots. She included photographs from our farm, on horseback; from my parents' home with our Akita puppies strewn around the hem of my gown; lawn shots stretched out under a tree. We ladies met at Elaine's local studio to dress. Initial photos were shot there with our bouquets of fresh flowers the day of the wedding. She attended the rehearsal dinner as well as the reception. When completed, our wedding album filled *three* blue leather binders, a spectacular and extravagant sight to behold.

With our blessing, she chose favorites from each of the three albums for one sample album. She submitted it to the state competition. Though I am biased, I was surprised that she only won second place.

Elaine is the reason that we have a matching photo album that I use for a bedtime story for our daughter. Something that she would offer to young families was a "five-year album." You could purchase the binding to match your wedding album, and three sittings a year at locations of your choice. From the proofs, you could purchase the poses you wanted to include in your book. This five-year album would be a superb partner for any wedding album.

Extravagant on my part would be an understatement. Three albums for our wedding alone. Undeterred, Elaine and I came up with the plan to do a four seasons book at our farm. We cleared the acreage, built the structures and added such luxuries as electricity and water; the photos that document the progress of these years make the slow work seem to fly by in a barrage of colors. With "Promises Kept" in gold lettering, that book sits proudly framed between the bindings of our wedding to the left and our children's albums to the right.

If a photograph is worth a thousand words, those albums tell mountains more than my writings ever could. I try to include the spirit of what is captured there visually into the written and spoken word. Perhaps, in the telling, my daughter, despite her lack of vision, can enjoy our collection. Now those others, who may never see our rainbow of snapshots, may be able to get a glimpse of the joy, which the blessings, that they capture, hold.

Lloyd Fuge beams happily with his pregnant wife

CHAPTER TWENTY-SIX
Timely Delivery

One of the wonderful things about being a family physician can be Obstetrics. Expanding a family, bringing new life into this world is an awesome part of the training and responsibility for family physicians. I was thrilled that, in my capacity as a new, young doctor, I got to do many deliveries.

Many, many diverse situations come up during deliveries. The first infant I delivered, back in Philadelphia, was to a fourteen-year-old mother. This was her second child. Her twelve-year-old sister was there as her support person. Believe me, between the two of them, they knew a lot more than I did about birthing babies. It seemed a lifetime between that delivery and the ones at our local hospital.

Years later, as I would be running in to do deliveries from various locations for my young families, that memory would cross my mind more than once. There was the evening when I came in from dancing. High heels were not usual for me anyway, but the evening dress and spike heels I had on were not at all appropriate for doing a delivery. The sequins were quickly exchanged for scrub clothes. It didn't matter how messy or dirty they became. My bare feet were covered only with little surgical booties until one thoughtful nurse offered to let me use her extra pair of shoes. Otherwise, she thought, my feet would get too wet.

A rare daylight delivery occurred while I was playing softball. I came racing in, as tanned as I can ever recall being. Young doctors from three local hospitals had been competing in a little local tournament, sponsored by several drug companies. A good sporting event was a chance to meet colleagues, get some exercise and sunshine, bring our families, and get somebody else to buy the food. One of the sponsors was an asthma medication. Their slogan on the t-shirts for their team was "A great set of lungs." The pediatric programs had, "Breast-fed is best-fed." Those t-shirts were an odd sight. I came jogging in from the dusty softball field to do the delivery.

The most memorable time, I can recall was coming in from horseback riding, with my Daniel Boone deerskin jacket. Its twelve-inch fringe flapped in the breeze behind me as I dashed down the hallway. My young patient gasped, moaned and cried out, "Thank God it's the doctor!"

Her appalled mother, taking in the same sight of me, replied, "Oh, my God! *That's* the doctor?"

Moments such as these, and the responsibility that came with them, prompted Tom and me to look for a close place to live. A maximum of twenty minutes drive to the hospital from our residence was necessary for doing deliveries. I could be a bit of a danger on the roads, making that twenty-minute drive. I could have competed with many ambulance drivers. Mothers who are on their first delivery tend to labor slowly, but after a mom had two or three babies, things could go lickety split. To arrive in time to help, I needed to figure out ways around railroad tracks, bridges, and other local traffic. To minimize the NASCAR-like events, we looked for our ten acres of heaven, in a tight circumference around my community hospital.

We saw property from the sublime to the ridiculous. There was one piece of land, thirty-nine acres, on the top of a mountain. The realtor explained that it was "perfectly flat up there." How they could tell that, I don't know. There was no path, let alone a road for the steep climb to the top. Perhaps helicopter?

Another was a falling-down shack on fifty acres. "Free natural gas" read the ad. Someone crazier than us bid on it.

A sixty-acre plateau at the top of a precipitous drive had a very dangerous entrance. The land had pretty much been raped and pillaged. The road frontage, mineral rights and even the topsoil had been sold off. There was no accessible water. You get the idea. The sellers also wanted a small fortune for it.

Sellers' prices could be quite unrealistic. One thirty acre plot was on the market for more than a million dollars. Some had old, partly-torn down structures. One had an old arena. Lots had trailers. Others had no structure or utilities at all. There were grass and weeds, and rarely trees.

Finally, there was a lovely little valley, hidden from view of the roads, just eight miles, from the hospital. The land hadn't been surveyed for more than a hundred years. The original documents spoke of rods and perches, rather than feet and inches. It measured from "so and so's stump" to "this or that fence," long since disappeared. The price of "the land and what came on it," which included a small farmhouse, was reasonable. Could we get a good rate from the bank? Would we get a survey done in time? We weren't sure, but it certainly met the criteria of being close enough to the hospital, so the race began.

We gave up our honeymoon to pursue our farm. I negotiated with the bank. An extension on the good mortgage rate would make it possible for us to manage the cost. This cute little farmhouse had been built by a plumber for his family. There were four bathrooms in it, lots and lots of stuff to wash. (I wasn't particularly fond of housework.) Negotiations through the realtor got the price lowered because I didn't plan on spending my life cleaning porcelain and windows for nothing. Tom cattle-prodded the survey team. In the early part of spring, they worked around trees and fallen debris from the recent winter, to find remnants of that old fence referenced in the historical deeds.

We "closed" at midnight on the last day of our extension from the bank for the mortgage. The survey people didn't finish drawing up the materials from their survey until the next day. They only had until the close of business at the courthouse to register the papers in downtown Pittsburgh, or the sale would have been void.

I got sheets for our honeymoon, a lovely bedding set. We had no furniture, so we slept on the floor. We will always have the sheets from our first night together, as a very special memento from our honeymoon.

Promises Kept Farm became our new home, located close enough to the hospital so I wouldn't break a promise to the mothers who would need me or the patients who would be under my charge. Tom told me he would get them to finish the survey in time, just another example of the fact that he had never broken a promise to me. When it came time to register our farm corporation's name with the State of Pennsylvania, it became officially "Promises Kept Farm."

**The logo for LHF's practice was a red apple
and so a collection began***

CHAPTER TWENTY-SEVEN
Friends and Acquaintances

I returned to Western Pennsylvania to be close to my family and because I had found an excellent Family Practice Residency. While I was completing those three years in Monroeville, I was fortunate to have several opportunities to do part-time work. They gave me the chance to serve the community and earn extra money to start repaying the enormous financial debt that could burden decades of my future. Even better, I could try to find the right niche, a place where I would spend my career.

At one point, there were a total of nine locations where I was spending some time each week, working in various capacities as a physician. I started out by doing an evening a month in a tiny little free clinic in New Kensington, Pennsylvania. Patients gave a donation if they could. I coordinated that location for six or seven of my colleagues so that together, we covered several days every month and expanded the services offered to the community.

Next, I added two entrepreneurial local physicians' offices. They were very different. First was a young graduate of Shadyside. He started offices in three locations surrounding Monroeville. He offered evening and Saturday hours. In his little empire, others worked for him. Second, a senior clinician had arranged with a local hospital for a building with more than a dozen exam rooms. He personally coordinated care for twelve hours a day, Monday through Friday, plus some hours Saturday and Sunday— more than three hundred and sixty days a year. He hired young clinicians to cover three or four hours a day. Who knows, perhaps that was when he rounded at the hospital or even slept. The office scheduled visits for six to eight patients an hour, plus walk-ins. He did X-Ray and laboratory work. I was an addition for providing female gynecology care. The first had modern equipment, carefully laid out scheduling, and dictated office notes. The latter had three by five inch cards as records, with only a diagnosis, anything pertinent you wanted to remember about the case, and the fee that would be charged.

To this eclectic combination, I added some weekend rounds on local hospital patients for MGG Corporation's female internist. She was so dedicated and methodical that she could spend as many as twelve hours or more in just one of the two or three facilities where they were to see patients daily. I enjoyed seeing the Forbes Hospital patients.

Other opportunities were more random, like a couple of hours at the local cancer center. The site could not be run without a physician present, in case of any problem with a patient. The pampered Radiation Oncologist, a sub-specialist who did the X-Ray treatment for those with cancer, took a two-hour dinner break. Sitting in for him those two hours, I got paid well while reading my journals and educational material. I was also a physician backup for the local sports center. They did rehabilitation exercise for people after heart attacks. The job was to monitor if a member's heart rate was safe and provide cardiac care in case of any catastrophes. I learned about exercise, got a chance to use the equipment free, and was paid a little for my time. A local HMO (Health Maintenance Organization) was just forming called Health America. They had regulation appointment slots of fifteen to thirty minutes. If they needed additional slots staffed, they would pay a young physician as much as one hundred dollars an hour. There was no notice. Whenever I had free time, I would put my name on the list for consideration.

Each opportunity gave me new insight into a different type of patient care and a different type of work experience. They gave me a foundation from which to select where I would work later. Hard work during my residency paid off when I was elected by the young physicians and faculty to be the Assistant Chief Resident in my second year. Subsequently, I was voted Chief Resident in my final year. The Chief Resident's position actually paid one thousand dollars for the year. It afforded me the opportunity to lead by example, to intervene in clinician disputes, to present teaching topics to other young doctors in training, and to work with a wide variety of doctors as a colleague.

Both local clinicians, the HMO and the multi-specialty group, MGG, all offered me jobs. I selected MGG, because it afforded me the most autonomy. Initially, it did not pay the best, but I was advised that the more I worked, the more the financial reward would be. It was what they called: an "eat what you kill" system. It rewarded me well over the years for my tireless efforts.

My negotiations for the contract were simple. I explained that I would require four weeks' vacation. I had that in training and would not consider less. I apologized for wasting their time, when they were planning for me to have only one or two, and stood to leave. The lead physician, RER, called after me. He said that my vacation request was not a problem and slashed out the previous offer. He handwrote in, with his fountain pen, four weeks, and initialed it. I will always remember those initials. They sealed the deal that determined a decade of my life. I was set for the next ten years. It was a standing joke among my friends and family that in those ten years, I did not take four weeks of vacation combined! But, they were mine for the asking, if I chose.

MGG had arranged for me to start in a small, local office with a senior clinician in General Practice who was looking to decrease his hours and retire. Dr. Hendry was a gentleman. The word completely described his demeanor, his attire, and his handling of situations, both personal and clinical. Over his dozens of years of practice, he had carefully screened and cultivated a group of patients who were both appreciative of their physician's efforts and considerate of his time. They rarely called, even for an emergency. It was my privilege to work in this peaceful and positive environment at the start of my private community practice. The staff was hand-picked and accommodating, deferential and respectful of their physicians, competent and efficient in their work. In this sublime environment, I made many acquaintances. April was often the month of great events in my life, not just my birthday. In April, that first contract for employment was finalized. In April, Dr. Hendry reported that he was retiring completely, shortly after the announcement that we would be refurbishing the offices. An additional thousand square feet was finished to better accommodate our enlarging patient population.

Though I was blessed to eventually take over the practices of two local family practice physicians, one in Monroeville and one in Murrysville, it was this original group which set the framework for the collegial interactions I would have in the future.

I was careful never to speak of who I was taking care of as a patient, even to their neighbors or family. I've often thought, over the years, that it was that staunch adherence to complete confidentiality, as much as my capability for clinical care that brought friends, and even family, to request me as their physician. They could rely on the fact that no one would know I filled that capacity, unless they said so.

Over the last twenty years in medicine, I've had many acknowledgements of the care and compassion that I have shared. I have occasionally thought I was living in a different time, when the barter system for my services would have been the norm. That simpler time would have been an interesting one in which to live. I'm sure I would not have gone hungry, under that system, though I appreciate the technology and wonders of our current age in medicine. I have been blessed with many mementos. Each thank you, whether by hug or tear, note or package, was special to me. These acquaintances have grown to be like family, by giving me the privilege of knowing them and their loved ones, by sharing with me their joys and troubles. I have been truly blessed.

On occasion, an especially unusual memento would come my way. Dr. Hendry had a solid steel door, locked between the patients' waiting/receiving area and the front desk, a bastion of security between the clinical area and the local community. It had a tiny sliding window where staff sat inside the security door. A young, single, construction worker brought a long-stemmed rose and a note. My nurse accepted it graciously. It read: "There are eleven more waiting on a table at Christopher's. Let's get them together tonight." Sandy answered that one for me, simply by saying that she'd have to check with my husband! She "wasn't sure that I'd be free." It would seem that some acquaintances were more intent on being friends than others.

**Family and friends do the weekend barn raising
for Promises Kept Farm***

CHAPTER TWENTY-EIGHT
Two Hundred Feet Restriction

I never saw the rest of those roses, but having a construction contact proved useful when we needed a backhoe to prepare land on our new farm for a barn — a curiously urgent project necessitated by some small print, on the contract for our new home. Apparently, the phrase, "remaining mineral rights staying with the property we purchased" meant such things as copper, silver, gold, or uranium. It did *not* include the coal which had been mined out from under most of our community.

More importantly, the gas and oil rights had been

bartered off at the last minute by the former owners, presumably, with the hope of royalty payments that would sustain them as income in the future. Unfortunately, that left us, the new owners, to deal with the gas and oil company. They came to survey their new rights when my young husband, Tom, a victim, if you will, of a gas company injury, was home. I imagine it was not a friendly greeting for the survey crew, unexpected and unwelcome, on our new farm. They left, but returned with reinforcements and documentation.

It actually required calling in some favors to get an audience with an attorney who specialized in fighting gas and oil companies in our area. The audience came with a price tag of four hundred dollars an hour for Brown Esquire Services. We learned that there were pitifully few restrictions to what a gas and oil company could do to your property and where. We were advised that we had neither the time nor the money to devote to fighting such a powerful adversary. They could drag us back and forth to court at any inconvenient moment, require me to cancel patients, leave work, lose income, with little more than a week's notice. It could drag on proceedings for months or years. At the huge amount per hour for an attorney, it was easy to see the point that was being made.

We learned that there were three restrictions about where the stinky, noisy, and unsightly oil well could be placed on property. It had to be at least three hundred thirty feet in from the boundary of the property itself. It had to be at least two hundred feet away from an inhabited structure and one hundred feet from a water source. Our property was pretty much the shape of our Pennsylvania Keystone State, with a little enlargement in the rectangle at the northwest corner, where the house stood. There was a creek that ran through a portion of the property, and a five hundred thousand gallon pond near one of the corners.

Still, allowing for those limitations, there was a band down the middle of our property that the gas and oil well company could utilize. Their chosen spot: in our lovely valley where our home's huge picture windows and balcony overlooked, some two hundred ten feet away, downwind.

To fight or not to fight this gas and oil company and their plans to put their monstrous rig forever in our scenic view, was the question. Over this, Tom & I fought. My husband stormed out of the house and jumped on our utility quad. So violent had been our verbal exchange that I was not sure where he would go, or if he would return. I dashed out of our home as he gunned the engine and jumped up behind him on our four-wheel drive Kawasaki, affectionately called our "first cow" on the farm, and hung on for dear life. He sped, not speaking, not looking back, over the rough terrain and steep grades of our beautiful Promises Kept farmland. We did not wreck. We did not speak. I did not fall off. He eventually came home. That was a truly frightening ride. I prayed and cried. When we came home, we slept fitfully, but arose to make a plan of attack *together*.

They would be coming soon down the same access drive we entered from the street and onto our grass-covered path. There was not a good shelf there, flat enough for their rigs to find purchase. This was an area of virgin ground, which had not been undermined by coal. There was not much time, perhaps a week or less when they would arrive. We could think of only one restriction that could hold the powerful oil company at bay, one possible safeguard against them plopping their monstrous malodorous machine smack in the middle of our pristine scenic valley. The law does *not* allow them to build and drill within two hundred feet of an inhabited structure. We needed a barn to bring our horses here eventually anyway. We had just a week, could we erect one in time?

Tom and I had been hoping to build next to our house on the other side in our little yard. We both owned horses that were being stabled elsewhere. It would be a start to have them close to home. On the flattest land close to our home would have been ideal. They would be easily accessed regardless of weather and convenient to saddle quickly for short rides. We changed our location plans to the valley that the gas and oil company desired to use. We called my construction friend, the one of the roses, to bring his backhoe and clear enough of the embankment in the valley to make a level patch. He came and left quickly. The mound of dirt removed from the hillside, was left piled loosely in the middle of our new plateau. It seemed as I stood at the base of it, that it towered as high as our little farmhouse.

Now *we* would plan for the beautiful valley. As the backhoe left us a monster dirt pile to remove, we finalized the arrangements for the building materials to be delivered. Morton Lester had a new combination facility with specialized siding, which would not leave crawl spaces for rodents. Walls would be divided in half, so any livestock that kicked or damaged the lower portion would afford us the opportunity to remove that one lower panel and replace it. There were safety features, like bird netting along the eaves to allow better ventilation and not allow access for the winged creatures. Special grooves in the ridges of the roof were designed to keep out nesting insects like wasps. Crowned by a light-colored roof, to maximize cooling for the summer, with built-in skylights, our stable could be illuminated even without electricity. The building would be a wonder, with stalls that could be divided in different sizes for various reasons. For breeding and calving, the animals could be afforded a larger space, later divided to safely separate the maturing young from the parents. Our state-of-the-art dream barn was financed through a small home equity loan and would be delivered before the weekend.

A small skid loader was the only equipment Tom could arrange during the week to start moving the mound of loose dirt out of the way. It seemed a monumental task. I took my portable phone, in those days, an enormous contraption about the size of a briefcase, and our only shovel, a small spade for the garden, down to help. The only thing I had to haul the dirt in after shoveling it was my tall kitchen garbage can. So, in between my beeper ringing and calling patients in need, I shoveled and dragged. Tom steered and lifted one skid-loader full after another, day into night, by flashlight and headlight, for any waking moment at home, to be ready for the weekend.

Not married until his thirties, over the years, Tom had helped many with the carpentry work on their remodeling, new roofs, whole homes, extended garages or mountain cabins. When he put out that urgent call for assistance, some thirty-three families descended on our little homestead that precious weekend, before the gas and oil company could begin their demolition.

Over the years, my mother had supported my father's political ambitions by cooking for many events from family gatherings to community days, to big political rallies, dishpans full of macaroni salads and enormous pots of barbecued ham sandwiches. Mom and Aunt Lynn facilitated food preparation for the many helpers of that weekend, while I ran between them and Tom and the men, who came to help their friend. I brought beverages, called for mealtimes, and took photographs of the modern barn raising. When it was all said and done, we had a beautiful, state-of-the-art, inhabited structure, just two hundred and ten feet below our home, in our scenic valley, where the gas and oil company had hoped to dig. The barn was a testament to our determination and creative problem solving, brought to completion by friends and acquaintances to whom we will be eternally grateful.

Sikira was loosing her vision, but still watched a toy move

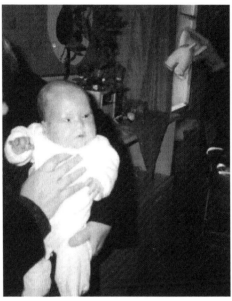

CHAPTER TWENTY-NINE
The Bedtime Story

Once upon a time, far, far away, in a little country called Croatia, there was a beautiful little princess with no name. The little "Princess" was going blind. One day, her fairy godmother, Miss Colleen, told a nice lady and a nice man named Tom and LaDonna about the little princess. They got on an airplane and flew all the way across the Atlantic Ocean and rescued the little princess and brought her home with them to live at Promises Kept Farm.

There was a great gathering of friends to greet the little princess as she landed in the United States, even though it was the middle of the night. Everyone was so excited to see her for the first time. When she got to her new home, there was Kodiac, an Akita guard dog to keep her safe, and a lovely little music box that played "It's a Small World."

The lady and the man were happy to have that little princess as part of their family, but something was missing; she needed a name. They dressed her in a beautiful gown of white and took her to St. Elizabeth's Church with Grandpap Hun and Aunt Michaelette to be her Godparents. As they put the special water and oil on her little head, she clasped her little hands together, as if to pray. The family was so happy together. Whether that special little princess needed extra medicine or extra care, her new mommy and daddy went with her to every hospital test, surgery and doctor.

There were so many wonderful parties, all the people wanting to welcome our little princess. She had many cakes, one with a special little baby doll in the center, one with a merry-go-round of animals, one cake with a horse on it, one with a cross and a prayer. There were dozens of gifts and a hundred different outfits. A special music box played "Lullaby and Goodnight." There were stuffed animals that made noise when you squeezed them. There was a swing that rocked back and forth, back and forth. All the cheering and clapping made the little princess happy.

She always smiled and clasped her little hands together in front of her. There was so much to do and learn. She learned to swallow. She learned to make noises and speak. She learned to sit. Finally, she learned to stand. She blew bubbles and wore special big glasses to help her precious eyes.

She sat on the horses and tapped them with her tiny feet to make them walk. She waved and she threw her hands up in the air to say, "I'm soooo big!"

"How big?"

"Soooo big!" She tapped on the keys on Grammies' piano. She rocked on the rocker with Grandma Nancy. She chewed on Mommy's little pewter necklace of mare and foal. She got her first little teeth.

She had fairy princess birthdays: lamb rotated on a big spit to celebrate how happy everyone was to have her. She got roses and a beautiful crystal vase each year. A huge banner spelled out: "Happy Birthday Sikira." Awesome carvings of horses made out of enormous blocks of ice were surrounded by flowers from the gardens. There were baskets of carnations and collections of streamers and balloons.

The beautiful princess was named Sikira Marie. Sikira had her own playground. At the farm, she had a special swing and an awesome cedar deck, the slats so close together so nothing would sneak out and away from her. There were rides on the tractor and the little garden parties in the flowerbeds with her dolls. She had her own little sprinkling can, a glider with handmade quilts, horse jackets and a running stroller. There were buckets of water she brought for the animals. She had kittens in the gazebo. Tiger and Meow, Mickey Mouse, and Shelly. There was an arbor for roses. She had a playhouse with a phone and kitchen. Sikira played with Akita puppies. She felt raised-letter signs for the farm and her last name.

Sikira enjoyed a petting zoo, with potbellied pigs, chickens, goats, ducks, and donkeys. Cousin Luanna joined our happy family. The princess would meet other special people, including Shania. She got to hold a live tiny owl and a young hawk. The most wonderful part of all was that one day, our special little princess would have a baby brother and our family would be complete. The end.

Sikira was always a good sleeper. Sometimes, it seemed she slept more than she was awake. Our bedtime rituals, when she was young, were perhaps more for me than for her. Now, as the years have gone by, they seem to be engrained.

We were not a family who had the nightly bath with giggles and bubbles and bed. My daughter, who loves water, perhaps would have enjoyed that better. We were limited by her hypersensitive skin never to do bubble baths, and to wash as infrequently as once or twice a week. When we deviated from that tough prescription of water avoidance, her skin would dry, crack and even bleed. Our evenings were instead time for stories.

My special lullaby growing up had been Brahms' "Lullaby and Goodnight." It was my favorite, and I think until I left for college, my mother sang it to me each night. We included that song in our nightly ritual with our daughter. But our highlight was something different. Our special storybook was called "Why Was I Adopted?" Written for a child to understand, we read it several nights a week. A small paperback by Carole Livingston. It became a way to share that special concept of joining a new family. I added one crucial extra sentence: "Adopted means loved twice." That phrase was parroted by my children at very young ages.

Other evenings, we told a story about Sikira, herself— the tale of how we found her, flew to Europe to get her, and brought her home to be our pride and joy. With her picture book as a guide, we made the tale up new each time of its telling. We looked at the pages of an enormous leather-bound photo album entitled Sikira. Most of the thirty pages were eight by ten color photographs, but some held special panoramas. I used this personalized masterpiece to stimulate Sikira's mind to what her eyes *could not* see: bright colors, large faces, and personalized topics. I narrated her story with the loving remembrances of bringing her into the arms of our family. The book included collages of our simple photos taken in Croatia during our whirlwind trip, with a panorama of our living room the night before her first surgery, following her midnight arrival at the local airport, greeted by friends and her personal photographer. Photos chronicled her christening and the lavish celebrations of her first four birthdays, as we joyously commemorated the gift of her presence in our hearts and our home.

*Sikira sleeps on the plane trip back from Croatia

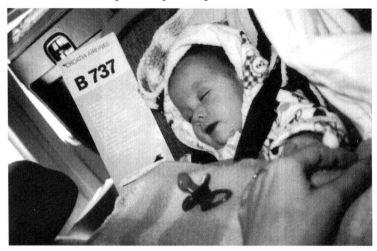

**Lithuanian Nana cuddles
new Croatian great-granddaughter, Sikira***

CHAPTER THIRTY
Lifeboat

Ask most people about adoption and they'll tell you it is a long, drawn out, arduous process. Those who pursue international adoptions may wait one to three years doing paperwork and getting permissions. Tom and I ended up doing a whirlwind of an overseas adoption in under two months.

Tom and I were not thinking about adoption exactly; we were thinking about a family. My girlfriend, Colleen and I were talking about how hard it is to get any infant nowadays, let alone a healthy one. We pondered about what difficulties we would be able to manage in an infant of our own. She thought she might be able to figure out hearing and orthopedic troubles. "After all, you could operate or do therapy for those." she said. I was sure that deafness would be tougher for me, but that blindness would be more manageable because of my upbringing with my blind parents. Not long after, Colleen heard about an infant in Croatia who was losing her vision. Croatia had regulations against removing children from the country. They considered them "resources." There was actually a way to send funds into the country to help take care of a child there; however, in 1994, there was a war going on. Bosnia, Croatia, Lithuania, Serbia—that whole area was in turmoil. The financial structure of the government was struggling. They were in the process of changing over what kind of money they had to use. Like the South, when the United States won the Civil War and Confederate dollars were suddenly useless, the "old" Croatian paper currency was scrap. The head of the orphanage, in Zagreb, the capital, thought that an exception might be made for urgently needed medical care that was unavailable in Croatia.

Colleen called me. I was at work. Colleen asked if Tom and I wanted this precious baby girl, rapidly losing her vision. It was likely retinopathy of prematurity, preventable here these days and possibly correctable with surgery available for her in Pittsburgh, if started in time. I cried. I was sure that Tom would say "no." I would have to go home to ask this one. This would *not* be something to ask him over the telephone.

As expected, his initial answer was "no." When we went to church, I waited until he was done praying. I asked what he had prayed for. "A baby," came Tom's expected reply.

"What do you pray for every day?" "A baby," Tom reiterated.

"Well, this *is* a baby! You are sounding like the drowning man who turns away the lifeboat because God is going to save him. She could be our baby."

"Maybe."

That was all I needed to hear to put the wheels into motion. All the training that I had in working on critical things when sleep deprived, all my work relationships and all the contacts my family and I had made over three generations growing up with a Lithuanian Nana in a town steeped in Croatian heritage came together in the next thirteen days. I did not sleep. I called and prayed and wrote.

In days, we accomplished months of paperwork. We bypassed years of red tape. We accomplished miracles. With a renowned eye surgeon standing by, agreeing to operate, we got INS to agree to allow the baby into the U.S. With FBI intervention and 24-hour U.S. mailers, we were "walked through" fingerprint reviews and Child Safety checks. Unrelated local people we did not even know and friends alike helped by staying late, getting up early, writing references, doing our adoption physicals, translating documents into Croatian, and taking photos for passports. They got Tom approved to travel internationally for medical rescue, without even a birth certificate. They got me coverage for work. My boss arranged for us to have the five thousand dollars, for tickets guaranteed to and from Croatia, for two of us to go and three to return. Our State Representative hand carried our documents to Harrisburg to have the State of Pennsylvania's stamped acknowledgement on our notaries' signatures certifying all of our documents as authentic. As it was Easter, he had to have an official "named" to be able to get the necessary seals over the holiday.

The local agents at AAA made rotating travel arrangements every day to be prepared for when our visa to travel into Croatia would come through. The country was under terrorist watch. Travel was only allowed from one of three cities: Frankfort, Moscow or Paris. You could only land in one city in the whole country and there only two days a week. Fortunately, that city was Zagreb, the capital, and our destination.

When everything was in place, we prayed, waited, and

tried to work, sleep and take care of each other. I wrote a journal. Tom found people to take care of our farm when we would be called. Our bags were packed. We tried to be calm.

I was at work when the call came. If we could be at the airport in an hour, we could go. I left patients in their exam rooms waiting to be seen. My staff went in to tell them that the doctor had left the country. My nurse practitioner would come over from another office to see them if they wanted to wait—or they could reschedule. Dr. Fuge had gone to rescue a baby. Everyone was gracious. I was not sure whether there would be indignation at my return. I did not worry about it as I rushed to meet Tom. On return, in fact, there were congratulations, banners and well wishes.

There has not been a wonderful moment in my life that, I can recall, when I did not get my period. This was no exception. On the way to the airport, I had Tom stopping at a convenience store for supplies: peanut butter, crackers, a book to read during the twenty-four-hour trip, and *tampons*.

Though we traveled by plane, I had time to think back on my lifeboat analogy. Tom had transformed from cautious. Tom had worried that we would get attached, only to have something tear our new family asunder. Now he was anxious and optimistic. We might be this baby's lifeboat but she, in a way, would be ours. I was sure that our life would not be complete without her.

Upon our return, as we waited in the hallway of Children's Hospital's surgical suites for word from our new daughter's eye surgeon, Tom and I addressed more than one hundred thank you notes, worded as follows:

Sikira, Tom and I are writing to thank you.

Though exhausted from the return 20-hour and four plane ride trip, we had to pause to send this quick note to you. Whether you helped expedite U.S. paperwork, picked up the pieces of our lives as we rushed off on our whirlwind trip to Croatia or graciously shared food, supplies, time, well wishes or prayers – you have been part of a miracle. You have given us a daughter. You have given her the chance for sight and perhaps most importantly, you have given her a home, a home with love. You have shared your love. You have given her a chance.

As we see each of those who gave of themselves to make this possible in the weeks and months ahead— know that your kindnesses are forever remembered in our hearts and Sikira's diary. Because of you, the Spring of '94 will always be known as a season of hope.

Gratefully yours,
Tom and La Donna
Adopted Parents of Sikira Marie
God Bless.

**Sikira and Tom sleep peacefully together,
on a mat on the floor, in Croatia***

CHAPTER THIRTY-TWO
Croatia

United Nations uniformed troops with weapons were at the airstrip in Croatia when Tom and I landed. Our passports were confiscated by the officials there to meet us. We could stay at a "safe house" until all was arranged. We had been warned to bring cash. Local support services could be limited by the conflict in the area. "Don't worry," they told us. "The fighting is thirteen *whole* kilometers away." Tom assured me that he would get a money belt and put it under his t-shirt.

I was concerned that waving our American passports would be painting a target on us that said "shoot here to get rich." "They'll take it off your cold dead body," was my reply.

Seventy American dollars for our room, a mat to sleep on and access to the restroom down the hall; food was extra. Whatever they got from the market that morning would be the menu. It didn't matter to me what they called it; I could not understand the words and probably did not want to know. Seven-ounce orange sodas could be purchased still sealed in glass bottles. I had almost drunk them up to a current expiration date by the time we left. Our eight day stay dragged on, a little less pleasant because

I had foolishly left our toiletries in the restroom down the hall, and someone had quickly removed what we had brought with us. Thank goodness I still had my feminine products.

Once we picked up the little one from the State Orphanage, we had to go to the United States Embassy to meet with the Consul. He would give the final approval of our adoption from the U.S. standpoint. We made quite a procession; with the baby in the heavy, approved traveling/car/plane seat, I led the parade.

There was a pecking order to the proceedings. The Americans came first. Tom followed me, loaded down with our luggage, my medical supplies and even my butt bag. Next came the Croatian officials, the better the title, apparently, the closer to the front of our single-file line. Last was our translator, relegated to the end of the line, and completely unable to render any assistance to us at the front. Our little girl and I went through rather quickly, then we were locked into a small anteroom with no chairs to await the rest of the party. As I grew tired holding her and the bulky baby seat, I fretted, ached and finally leaned on a wall, wondering where Tom was, and what was taking so ridiculously long? Thirty minutes later, I was fuming!

Meanwhile, back isolated in the inspection room without a translator, Tom was trying not to get shot. We were told the baby's birthday. She had been premature, only two pounds and two ounces at birth. Croatia tracks weight in grams, not ounces. To figure out how much formula is needed to feed an infant of a specific weight, the formula companies make a device that calculates ounces of food based on the child's size. The mechanical device distressed the armed inspectors, so they confiscated it. The new thermometers that go into an infant's ear were unheard of to them. The fact that ours had a trigger button that you were to pull to get the reading was alarming; they did not want it demonstrated next to their heads! It too was carefully removed from our supplies and then from the room. Next came the most crucial items from my butt bag – *tampons*. Suspicious cylinders; when partly opened, an incriminating white cord fell down from the item . . . primer cord for an explosive device? Tom was sure they considered it, since they raised their weapons and stepped back from him. Desperately, he tried to pantomime an explanation. "You know, for women," he made an hourglass shape in the air. "Once a month." Tom held up one finger, hoping for understanding. "You know, they insert them." He gyrated his pelvis back and forth, motioning with his closed hand toward his groin. Since, those female supplies were not worth his life, he finished with, "Just keep them!"

We have laughed many times about this incident, since returning home. I did not laugh that day. I scolded him for taking so long, like he had any choice and yelled about his giving away my needed protection. The town was supposedly celebrating their nine hundredth year anniversary. Banners could be found throughout the town, but toiletries were in more limited supply.

Obviously, we made it home safely. However, I was irrevocably traumatized by it all. A full decade later, when Tom and I were going to take the whole family to Florida to visit Disney World for our daughter's tenth birthday, I demanded that we drive. No more planes, limited luggage or confiscating of my medical supplies for me. Tom graciously took two to three days to drive each way, stopping at countless rest stops along the way, to accommodate me. I had learned a few things, though. For instance, I never left our toilet paper unattended.

Massive twin oak tree overhanging our farm house*

CHAPTER THIRTY-TWO
The Tree

In the early days, as we'd be driving down the dirt and gravel paths on our new property, I found that we were talking with each other about everything and nothing. Topics ranged from events of the day to the weather, how beautiful the land was, how much we cared about each other, hopes for the future and plans for tomorrow.

Over the years, I have learned a few lessons the hard way. Whether from medical training or life's experience, I have found talking with each other to be useful. In relationships, over time, often we stop sharing that joyful, sometimes silly, sometimes intense banter that we have at the start of wonderful relationships. We become quiet with each other. We give up sharing our thoughts. We stop giving our partner the opportunity to vocalize and share theirs. Whether it's thoughts or feelings, opinions or possibilities, communicating is crucial. It can certainly be tough to be open and honest. Our inner thoughts and feelings may not be appreciated. We could be hurt.

It's such a wonder to know that we are accepted. Maybe

that's one of the things about prayer. We're never put down in prayer. Maybe prayer can make it a little bit easier to talk with our partner who is here. The first blessing when *talking* is sharing the happy banter. The second is *listening*.

If we're sensitive to not having our thoughts and feelings, dreams and possibilities cut off, laughed at or not heard, others may be too. So, take turns. Take the chance to be silent. Listen to the gift others are giving us, when they share their words and feelings. The better we listen, the more trust is built.

Honor your partner. Honor your husband. Honor your wife. In many weddings, the words "honor" and "obey" are removed from the vows. I, myself, would have been appalled at the concept of saying that I would "obey" my husband as part of our wedding service, but I've come to know many meanings for the word "honor." It doesn't mean just to exalt, to put up in a high place. It means to appreciate and value.

For Memorial Day, we honor those who have given the greatest sacrifice for us in our country for our freedoms. We remember the sacrifice of their service and their life. Honoring those we love, who are still with us, is at least as important.

A Commandment says "Honor thy father and thy mother," and certainly, anybody who is asked might say that that means to obey them, but it's much more. It's to be appreciative. Acknowledge the gift of their love. They have cared for you. Remember all the things they do for you, that you want to say "thank you" for.

The third and final thing, I would recommend for relationships is to say "thank you." Thank you for all the big things like spending your life with us, trusting us, taking care of us; all the little things like clearing the table, saying we look pretty, driving wherever we're going, or any of those things that make it a little bit easier on us.

On an, early drive up to our Promises Kept Farm, we talked. As we pulled into the driveway, above us, on a little embankment was an enormous, beautiful oak tree. This oak was one of the landmarks of our old deed. All four of our arms together, reaching around the trunk would barely allow our fingers to touch. I took ecology studies in college, as extra biology credits towards the dream of medical school, and learned to estimate trees' ages.

This beautiful expanse that our Creator had shared with us was at least two hundred, if not two hundred and fifty, years old. Its boughs stretched over much of the acre of flat yard that surrounded the structure in front of us. We paused in our conversation to appreciate its splendor.

At the end of a short silence, Tom turned to me and declared, "That tree has got to go."

I was appalled. "What are you talking about? That's a beautiful expanse of nature! An awesome creation of God! A gift for us to have for all time! It's been here maybe longer than our country! It's a cornerstone of our property line. That's the point where our property intersects the next family's. There's a huge colored marker around the trunk to acknowledge that significance. What do you mean it's got to go?" The arguments spewed out of me like a torrent.

Tom, matter-of-fact and always thinking of safety said, "It could fall on the house."

Aside from the fact that it had stood the test of time, for, most likely, better than a couple of centuries, my heartfelt response was, "That's why we've got homeowner insurance."

My sweetheart's immediate reply: "But what if you're under it?"

Without a pause, I retorted, "It's over the kitchen, I'll never be there."

I never gave in. As was usually the case, Tom let me have my way.

We've shared this story many times, with humor, over the years that we've lived at our home. The oak's great expanse of leaves towered over us, delicate light green in spring, heavy dark foliage in summer, beautiful rainbow in the fall. I say "home," not "house," because of our history. We had sacrificed for it, fought for it, from bankers' meetings and survey struggles, to sharing our special sheets on the floors inside its walls. No longer a mere building, it was home, a place exemplifying our foundation of love and appreciation.

I was re-telling that story on June 30, 1998 at lunch to some of my coworkers. They were laughing, "Oh, how silly." "You cooking?" "You're hard at work, not there preparing meals . . ." We had a little chuckle. I would cook at least once a year, just to prove that I could. Thanksgiving, was my time to show off culinary prowess with two meats, six vegetables, and multiple salads.

The day had deteriorated from a soft rain, into a powerful storm. Upon returning from lunch break, the hospital and the office both lost their power. Backup generators didn't work. I was in an exam room with no windows, counseling a patient about his fears. Suddenly, we were in a blackened room together. I heard him gasp. I asked, "Do you happen to be afraid of the dark?" Fortunately, that lightened the mood with humor, until we could find a flashlight. We used the little one for checking ears to find our way to a door. The hospital patients were worse off. Staff took turns giving them oxygen by hand, one pump bag at a time. The laughter and lightheartedness of lunch was gone, washed away by the adrenaline rush of surprise and danger, concern and distress.

Concerned over the patients' care, the phone call from my sweetheart was not a welcome distraction. I don't recall who took the initial phone call, but she came to get me. I recall the conversation only in bits and pieces, as I was distracted by the crisis in my medical world. The first piece of the conversation that really sunk in was, "Find another place to live." He had such a rough tone to his voice. It was foreign to me. Taken aback, hurt, agitated, I took it to mean that he was telling me to leave, or not be with him.

In my shock and surprise, my response was, "Who is she?" thinking my world had come crashing to an end. Was I being replaced by someone else?

He went on about "taking our daughter" and "being somewhere else." Still, not really tracking, confused, I queried him further. He went on to tell that "Our Tree" *had* come crashing down on the kitchen. The house was gone. I needed to find another place. I thought he must know I had been telling our tree story at lunch. I was not amused. Who had he been talking with? I was going to be late to come home for dinner, again. He didn't need to fix anything. Things were bad here because of the storm, even a possible tornado in Monroeville! I was just not in the mood for being teased.

I don't know exactly what words I used to tell him all that, but I changed my tone of voice. I was not happy. That communication, the "listening" to what the other person has to say, *none* of that was happening. Therefore, unfortunately, it took me awhile to realize his call had nothing to do with that day's lunch humor. Tom's call was trying to relay the fact that the storm had been harsh throughout our area, a tornado they said, in several local communities.

"Microburst" is what they finally called it at our residence. A path of trees were snapped in half through our valley. Our tree, two hundred fifty years of perseverance, was snapped in half and came crashing down on our kitchen. Ninety tons of wood, they estimated, went crushing through the point of our roof over our kitchen. My sweetheart, just arrived home from a little hospital surgery on a shoulder injury. Tom was standing at the kitchen sink, getting a glass of water, looking out at the great expanse of our green beautiful tree, when it decided to come *in* for a visit. Thank God, he was all right.

We did have to find another place to live. It took the better part of thirteen months to completely rebuild that broken house back into a home.

There were miracles that day. Everyone was home but me; but everyone was fine. In fact, we had a sitter with my daughter, who was in her room at the time. Trees were down, all of them massive. The barn and the out buildings were spared. The tree actually fell across the kennels with all of the dogs in them. None of them were injured. Our home needed a huge amount of repair over quite an extended period of time, but another miracle was that so little else was damaged.

We have a cathedral ceiling on the one side of the living room. On it were massive framed portraits: our wedding, our first time at Promises Kept Farm, me on horseback with Tom beside me in a western duster. In that photo, I looked like "Dr. Quinn, Medicine Woman" of television fame. (In fact, friends called me "Dr. Quinn, Monroeville" after the adventures that we had in our little homestead farm.) Although water came pouring into our home through the cracked roof, none of the pictures were damaged.

Our dining room had been a gift from my husband and his family for our second anniversary. (The first anniversary is commemorated with paper. I got a crate of paper products from his family that first year. It took us years to use everything from wax paper to computer paper and feminine products.) The second anniversary is commemorated with wood. They changed the whole layout of our little farmhouse. The pantry, hallway and stairwell were all opened up, connected by oak banisters and crown molding around the ceiling, to create a formal, dining room. In my dining room, were two cherry wood china closets. They had slowly been filled by special pieces from our life together. We've celebrated on the thirteenth of *every* month, the day of our anniversary, with a card, a token, a special meal together or a flower, a piece of china or crystal. We have honored each other monthly and kept the fragile collection in that dining room. Not a single piece of wood or furniture, crystal or china was damaged—a true miracle, as the room was immediately next to the kitchen and its window faced our tree.

There were a lot of miracles that day. One such miracle was revealed during the clean-up efforts. Our great oak had a younger "sibling." A hundred-year-old oak stood just around the corner of our home, just next to our bedroom window. We saw it as we came into the carport or whenever we lifted our heads from our bed. I did not argue this time when Tom said that second tree had to go. When the workers worked on the tree undamaged by the storm, we found all but a two-inch circumference was hollow from twelve inches below ground to seven feet up the massive trunk! Surely, the other tree had to fall, because the angels were too busy keeping this one from crushing us in our bed, all these years. That day, I came to know that family was more important than any "thing," even than work.

Tom's wounded leg*

CHAPTER THIRTY-THREE
Haven From The Storm

Thunderstorms have had Tom's special attention, not because of the noise or the wonder or the power, like with our dogs and children, but because of the interesting, distressing, and inescapable fact that he could predict them. Our weathermen should be people who have suffered trauma or arthritis, as every area of injury seems to herald the approaching event with the intensity and fervor of the Second Coming.

The storm of June 30, 1998 was no different. Tom predicted that we would get hit hard because of his level of anticipatory distress, the exact moment and type of storm were still a mystery. The aftermath inevitably brought pain and increased difficulty with functioning. Walking was especially problematic for him. Before Tom and I had met, I would say, he tried to feed his leg to a piece of equipment. Tom would say he "had won the fight because he got to keep the leg." Humor does not really do the severity of injury justice.

The event happened off Galveston, Texas on one of the offshore oil rigs. Working on an oil rig was an excellent way to make a living. If you survived. Salaries were high, even for the least experienced workers, but benefits were few. The one "benefit" possibly appreciated by the crews was actually a convenience for the company. Companies had to fly all the men, equipment and supplies an extended distance off shore to the rigs. To limit trips, the crews would go out in two-week shifts. There would not be another transport until the end of that time for any reason. One perk was that you worked half the year, two weeks on, two weeks off, for a significant salary.

Workers used their time off in quite varied ways. Resting was not always on the agenda. Rabble rousing, bar hopping, fighting and bingeing were frequent. In fact, when the transports would land inside the protected fencing areas, local entrepreneurs would line up at the gate. First the prostitutes, then the bill collectors, and then those with other wares, from cold alcoholic beverages, all the way to new vehicles. Half of these youngsters were eager to spend their fresh pay. Others hurried off to family, friends, or second jobs. Tom rotated his onshore time between building homes for a small construction business he and a friend had started and riding fence line on his friend's family's ranch, for some two thousand head of livestock. Being on horseback in the open air seemed like a vacation to him.

The work on the rig was hard and dangerous. There were attempts at significant safety precautions. The jumpsuits, whole body outfits that the individuals wore when they were in the active work area, were thick, rigid, cumbersome, and designed to protect against the harsh elements and sharp equipment pieces. At the very edge of the working platform to drill for oil, workers would strap into harnesses like they were about to be dropped by parachute. The heavy straps circling their bodies and legs were hooked up to a catapult arm. Dressed up in that fashion, they stepped onto pressure plates in the floor of the rig and typed in their code that adjusted for their weight. The reason for this was that if there was an explosion, workers would be lifted up by the blast. If the weight on the plate changed a certain percent, the catapult arm would whip them by the harness out to sea in the other direction in an attempt to save their lives.

Tom was in his harness when the large chain used to attach drill bits together was inadvertently wrapped around his leg, but not felt in his heavy protective gear. When the machine started up, the chain moved his leg, and the pressure-sensitive catapult reacted the way it was designed. The harness wrenched his body in the opposite direction, effectively separating his leg at each joint.

I can't imagine the excruciating pain that that modern day rack must have inflicted. Perhaps he passed out or just kept screaming. He doesn't talk about it often and not in much detail. What he does recall, with anger, is that policy of not sending transport for any reason before that two-week shift was up. He lay in the infirmary until the routine run. I have teased and called Tom the "Six Million Dollar Man" because of the TV program that portrayed the high expense of rebuilding an astronaut who had a grievous injury. Health care was not on Tom's benefits list. Once back on dry land, the medical profession began the arduous task of rebuilding him. It's no wonder that, when we met, he didn't like doctors. He had come home from Texas to live with his parents and see the local orthopedic doctors.

I didn't tell him that I was a clinician. I said I did P.R. work for MGG Corporation, the abbreviation for the medical group where I worked at the time. I considered I did do P.R. work for them. I spoke positively on their behalf with the community. Of course, it eventually became evident that I was a doctor. Thank goodness that by then, he loved me despite it.

That MGG Corporation was just a block from the intersection in Monroeville, Pennsylvania, where a little local tornado had touched down on that fated June day. Much of the power was out for the surrounding communities. Traffic lights were gone. Debris was in the streets. The local businesses had no working phones, not because the phone wires were down, but because most of the phone services were electric.

Our friend, Lee, from MGG, traversed the brief, but difficult distance to the local motel at that intersection, to ask for a vacancy for this suddenly displaced family of three. We headed out in our four-wheel drive to find our place to stay the night. Our vehicles were designed for Tom to be able to get in without bending his leg. His favorite manual transmission had given way to the practicality of automatic. When we pulled into their lot, we took the better parts of two spaces. Tom slowly extracted himself from behind the wheel and staggered to their doors. The old injury made Tom appear to be on one of those post-rig binges.

The front desk attendant was helpful and thoughtful. Certainly a small refrigerator could be available once the power was back, for the baby's special food. They found a perfect room for us right at the end of the hall. If the baby cried or fussed, it wouldn't bother others and others wouldn't bother us. Not a problem, she said, just at the top of those stairs, on the *ninth* floor. At times like this, it's hard to have a sense of humor.

I would like to think that we graciously suggested an alternative. Perhaps we weren't quite as calm and kind as this later telling. They did find us a spot next to their laundry on the ground level. A window facing the outside let in ambient light enough for us to see our new surrounding. Dimly. Thus we moved into our new home for the next month. That first night, we slept well in our new home.

I recalled another refuge from years past. It was a haven from a different kind of storm, an emotional storm. A one-room apartment retreat from my first marriage seemed palatial now, compared to our hotel room for three. This time, I was not afraid, only nostalgic.

Sikira's luxury crib set with horse motif*

CHAPTER THIRTY-FOUR
Precious Beds

The Hampton Inn, I am sure, is a lovely haven for travelers, tourists, and business folks on their short journeys. I can tell you that our room seemed far too small for a family of three to live in for a month. There were some amenities. Room service changed the bedding after unexpected accidents. A port-a-crib was arranged for our daughter, who was fortunately petite for her age. She stretched diagonally across it with no room to spare. Our refrigerator, graciously arranged by the establishment was only two feet tall, with limited storage options. The little cold breakfast available each morning in the lobby was more appreciated in the first week, than by the fourth. Their indoor pool was far too much water for us. Our home, with its cracked open roof, had been flooded by rain.

With many damaged properties in the area, our insurance company took some time to come out and survey our damage. It took longer still to decide what they would do with the residence. What to do? Raze it to the ground and start over? Repair it and hope? While they pondered and vacillated, we traveled back and forth to feed our animals and check on their safety. I'm sure we would have had offers of assistance had we vocalized our distress more publicly. There was no power; therefore, no security system. We were concerned about the possibility of vandalism, even in our remote area. We suffered in silence, as those days and weeks dragged into months.

When Tom and I met, I was living in my car. But shortly thereafter, I had a small, one-room apartment on Route 30. I recalled often in years since that it seemed if I opened the door and stepped out too far, I might have gotten my toes run over by the traffic. In point of fact, there were actually a few parking spaces between the door and the road, but the speed of the traffic and its noise did not go unnoticed. When I first moved in, I did not have any furniture. Because of that, the small space seemed larger. There were a few pieces of miscellaneous college paraphernalia in storage that found their way to my little place. Eventually, my eclectic collection included a mattress on the floor, a bean bag chair, an ironing board with a sheet over it to act as a buffet, and an overturned laundry basket to act as a table. The apartment was located halfway between the hospital in Monroeville and my office near the Churchill Police Station. The owners let me pay the rent one month at a time.

Now, years later, I would have considered its location a plus and its small size, ample, compared to a hotel room. We were all anxious to get home. I tried to convince the insurance company to rent us an RV or a mobile home. With forty acres, we could certainly keep it temporarily on site. It would have bathroom facilities, a place to cook, and would be safe in case there was instability in the residence that was being evaluated for repair. In addition, we would be on site and could safely monitor the animals as well as our possessions. They declined this offer and arranged for a furnished apartment for us, some twelve miles away. A lavish two-bedroom, two-bath, at the racquet club, with all the amenities, also meant we needed to make multiple trips back and forth to our damaged residence every day to check on everything.

Long ago, in my old one-room apartment, I had only an old mattress on the floor for sleeping. Getting a bed was a dream of mine then. I had saved up a little money until a local store was having a sale on water beds. One price, any size. I carefully paced off the maximum measurements of the apartment. My plan was to get the largest bed that would fit. Footstep by footstep, I counted the length and breadth of each display model. Happily, the king size bed would just make it within my restrictions. One hundred fifty dollars later, complete with a set of sheets and a heater, I had my first real piece of furniture. I've often joked that, I could flush the toilet or turn off the stove without leaving my bed.

Following the storm, our four-year-old had scarce room to roll either right or left in the port-a-crib the hotel provided. She had been displaced in June. Her ardent wish for her October birthday was a real bed of her own again.

Tom enjoys bows and firearms*

CHAPTER THIRTY-FIVE
Gone Fishing

When Tom and I met, I didn't tell him much about myself. He was very clear about his own interests. Before we had ever gone out, he remarked, "I hunt. I fish. I chew snuff." If I couldn't take him "as is," we weren't going anywhere.

I knew only a couple of his friends, but I knew he loved fishing. A day fishing seemed a good distraction from our current stress. Trips to check on farm animals between our temporary apartment and our home under repair could be tiring. The family of one of Tom's old friends owned property along a local reservoir, a site with restricted access and good fishing. Since it was not far, I was glad when he said he was going fishing there—until night fell. The hours passed and he hadn't returned. Midnight came and he still hadn't returned. I went from missing him, to concern for him, to distressed with him.

In Clairton, the little town where I grew up, the Monongahela River flows past the town. It is one of the small handful of rivers in the world that actually flows north. My mother used to tell a story to distract us kids from the water emptying out of the tub:

> The water goes down the pipe, down the drain, down to the sewer, down to the Monongahela. The Monongahela goes up and up and up and bumps heads with the Allegheny River. At Pittsburgh, they form the Ohio River. It goes down and around, around and down and becomes the Mississippi. The Mississippi goes down around, around and down to the Gulf of Mexico and out to the Atlantic Ocean. Along come the storm clouds and suck up water from the Atlantic Ocean. Rain clouds bring it back to us. Rains come down here and we have water again.

The tub would be empty. We would go to bed quietly contented.

There was a different story told about that Monongahela River for the teenagers in town. Boys would joke about taking girls to the river for a date alone. In the evenings, along the banks of the Monongahela River, the boys would tell the girls there were "submarine races." (Submarines could not and did not go down that particular river.) If the female lacked interest in the Navy, boys might suggest "watching the fish." At night, you couldn't see much of anything, let alone fish. Still, occasionally, there was a gullible girl who fell for it. The stories made for great locker room humor, night "fishing expeditions" having nothing to do with a worm on a hook but rather with unhooking a bra.

Now, as midnight passed and my husband was still out "fishing," I was wondering who was fishing for what, with whom, where. By two o'clock in the morning, I could stand it no longer. I collected our daughter out of her temporary, new bed at our temporary apartment. I put Sikira in our vehicle and started off to our home at Promises Kept Farm, anticipating that I would find whatever "fishing" was going on at that location. If not, I would start out towards other locations where "fishing" might go on and find out exactly who was fishing for what.

The good Lord was with me on that dark night. Between two and three o'clock in the morning, I actually passed my husband's vehicle going in the opposite direction. In retrospect, the chances of actually taking the same route that he would, in my distress, frantically driving with our daughter, were actually small. His explanation was that he was "really fishing." I didn't really believe him. His good buddies later joked and laughed. "Tom? No, he wasn't with us."

It took quite some time for me to find out that people *did* truly fish for fish at night. We came close to our second-ever fight through that highly stressful time while our house on Promises Kept Farm was being rebuilt. Not so much that I didn't trust my husband, I didn't trust those who might be fishing for *him*. Tom's teased me about "fishing" ever since then.

Upside-down Sikira

CHAPTER THIRTY-SIX
Please

As Sikira was growing up, we made many visits to eye doctors, eye surgeons and hospitals to try to salvage her vision. It has always been difficult for me to take her to the eye doctor's. She was not able to "hold" her eyes open for the doctor to inspect the inside of the eyes where most of her damage was.

To visualize better, the Ophthalmologist would put drops into her eyes. The drops would dilate the center portion of the eye. Through the dilated pupil, the doctor would have a larger area to see what was happening on the inside of the eye. The stronger the medications were, the more obnoxious, toxic, and burning they felt. Children would put their hands up and tightly try to pinch their eyelids shut to prevent the burning drops from getting in. The eye doctor would have a parent hold the little one on their lap, head down, restraining her arms and legs. Office staff would use special little tongs that would pry and hold eyelids open, while the harsh drops were used.

Sikira got old enough to verbalize her distress. On one such visit, she asked the nurse at the eye doctor why they used those "bad, hurting drops." The assistant's abrupt response was, "To see better."

There was a little pause and, with a sniffle, Sikira asked, "Please, can I have some more?" My daughter had not understood that to see better was meant for the eye doctor and not for my child to appreciate the sights of her world. I've cried many times, thinking about that visit.

LHF and Tom at the hospital charity ball

CHAPTER THIRTY-SEVEN
My Bodyguard

There is no doubt in my mind that I would not have been able to accomplish what I have in my life without Tom. He has always said that he would stand in front of me to protect me, that he would stand behind me to catch me if I would fall, and he would always walk beside me. Often, he would add that, together we could accomplish anything I wanted, because he would always be there for me. He has sacrificed a lot in his own life to keep one more promise, of partnership for the road we would walk together.

In our first five years, there was not a day that we were apart. Even when I was on call. I rested easier because he was beside me through each night. No matter how many calls came in to disrupt our sleep, he got up with me. When a particularly cantankerous Emergency Room physician insisted for something seemingly silly, that I "must come now and see this patient," Tom would get up.

He would quietly get dressed and tell me, "That's okay. I'll drive."

There was a different tone in the conversation when Tom walked in ahead of me at two or three o'clock in the morning, to evaluate a situation. After confronting anyone who tried to give me a hard time, he stepped aside and waited quietly away from the medical scene. We had a rule not to discuss the patient for confidentiality's sake. I suspect that rule over the decades has made it possible for friends, family, and neighbors to feel secure and safe in seeking me out for their medical care. I certainly felt secure and safe in Tom's care.

In my early years in medicine, it was common, even expected, for a new business, medical company, or pharmaceutical division to invite a physician and his or her family to a social event or a special dinner. These outings were springboards to medical discussions about their products. A senior colleague of mine told me that he could have eaten out every night of the week, with or without family.

Tom and I enjoyed our private time together. Dressing up to some extent was expected for such outings, and we did not like dressing up much. Our preferences prompted me to decline most invitations. What occasionally motivated me to attend was to gather the groundbreaking information or to hear a colleague speak. Food was rarely my motivator.

One such rare night, we strode into a fancy restaurant, single file. Tom was behind me, after having held open the door. A muscular man, six foot one inch, with a beard, no smile on his lips, Tom's eyes seemed to penetrate every corner, missing nothing. As we were seated at the long table of discussion, Tom held my chair. My colleagues, all male, were already seated. A physician to my right, whom I did not know, exclaimed, "How interesting. We all bring our wives and she brings her bodyguard." Tom said not a word that night. He acknowledged the comment with a stiff, crisp, half nod in the individual's direction, before sitting beside me for our meal. Years later, when Tom would ask me why I ever married him, the fact that he made me safe was on that list.

I've pursued many medical roles over the years. Tom had not complained. "If that's what you want," was his repeated refrain. Building a medical practice up to three offices and three hospitals would have been plenty for most. It would be even more time-consuming to add teaching or administration.

A prospective administrator has to be diplomatic. If I wanted to serve, represent and lead in the medical community or medical staff, I had to be tactfully. As a teacher, I tried to both learn *and* share. Tom and I shared stimulating conversations at home about the nuances of political intrigue — but in public, he learned to support me silently.

There are many things that Tom gave up to support me. Tom's orthopedic injuries, surgeries and medicines made it difficult and painful for him to get around. Tom is not a complainer. Though it is difficult to get his swollen leg or a post-surgery shoulder into dressy attire, he tried for me. He missed family events and friends' weddings. He did not go away to hunt, travel, or fish. I'm sure he missed the camaraderie of these activities he loved and the friends of his youth.

Tom would shampoo his baby-soft, blonde hair, trim his unruly beard, give me one of his rare smiles and off we would go to my events. Like a wedding planner, I would strive to have each element of our involvement precise and perfect. I carried a plethora of items, just in case . . . extra medications for Tom, a comb and even makeup for myself. In our vehicle would be an extra pair of stockings and an extra pair of shoes. I checked out in advance the "approved" dress for a philanthropic polo event, to wear the exact shade of green and appropriate length skirt.

I was known to marshal even more resources into planning the attack of the event. Like Caesar or Alexander coming to conquer populations, I viewed each event as a political opportunity or strategic challenge. I planned how to cover the entire terrain of the event so as to meet and greet everyone possible. As they say, an Army moves on its stomach. The cooks are important in war. In medicine, at a hospital, the maintenance and security, cafeteria workers and operators are the crucial backbone on which the facility can function. I've strived to know and acknowledge each individual as crucial in their own right, not just the titled CEOs and officers.

Driving with Tom on one such campaign, I scrutinized his carefully-trimmed beard and mustache. Tom had done an excellent job. But as I sat beside him, I became bothered by another type of hair—his nose hair. Of all such silly things I have fretted over through the years, in retrospect, I think this one may have topped the list. Tom had a couple of unruly strands at one nostril. "Long enough to add to your head of hair," I teased, as he drove along.

"Well, just get them," he said, expecting me, as always, to have any measure of materials needed to accomplish primping. He was correct, of course; I had cuticle scissors that should take care of the job nicely. Cuticle scissors, for those of us who do not manicure our nails on a routine basis, are an interesting type of tool. I got my first pair from my Grandma Nancy. She used them with a sharp precision of a surgical instrument for everything from handling splinters and sewing threads to trimming skin tears and the actual cuticles they were designed for. Hers were strong, yet small, shiny and sharp. The pair that I had with me that night was not of the same caliber as Grandma Nancy's. They were pointed and petite, difficult to get your fingers in the holes of the handle, and probably could have used some sharpening.

I leaned across the front seat of our vehicle as Tom was driving. I attacked the unruly group of hairs that protruded annoyingly from his right nostril. Tom was distressed first by my stabbing him with the point inside his nose and nearly veered off the road. During that maneuver, I caught the longest of the hairs in the hinge of the scissors. "I'll get it!" he snapped. Tom's tone was furious and it drove me back instantly to my seat, leaving the offending tools dangling from his nostril hair. Today, I have to chuckle. He was not in a chuckling mood. I don't think he's let me near him with scissors since, at least not small ones. "Scalpels, yes," he has been quoted as saying, "Scissors, no." What price we pay for vanity.

LHF as Chairman of Family Practice

CHAPTER THIRTY-EIGHT
Change

One of my patients recently said that a fellow physician remarked that I was someone who had been in "the right place at the right time." That is probably true.

1997 brought upheaval to the local medical community of Pennsylvania. There were two entrepreneurial groups, both merging hospitals and physician groups into financially cohesive units. The fight between them, though new, resembled the most bitter, historical sports rivalry imaginable. Patients were in danger of being in the crossfire.

I had worked for the local community Medical Staff as the elected Chairman of all the Family Physicians since 1991. For me, each individual clinician's concerns were an opportunity to show fairness or facilitate better patient care. I was proud and appreciative of the acknowledgement of my efforts when I was voted to be an officer for the whole Forbes Medical Staff.

First serving as Treasurer for two years, I was hopeful of becoming Vice President and then eventually, President. The Nominating Committee of physicians selected me for Vice President. The Medical Staff all voted for me. The President that year was to be another Family Physician, but abruptly, he resigned when his group joined UPMC, University of Pittsburgh Medical Center and our hospital joined their arch rival, AHERF.

Suddenly, I was President! I needed to address the more than eight hundred physicians of Forbes, whom I would be representing. A few minutes hardly seemed enough to acknowledge the huge changes that engulfed our medical world, unsettling friendships and dividing loyalties. My goal was to emphasize that we could make a difference. We still needed to work together.

When we gathered for the Annual Medical Staff Meeting at the local country club to hear about the changes from the hospital administration and Board, I stood and spoke.

> A year ago, I was honored to receive the nomination of your Nominating Committee and your vote for Vice President of the Medical Staff. I was honored to anticipate that a year hence, I would stand here as the incoming President to Forbes. Changes intervened. Change in health care, change in our practices, change in the status of our institution, change in the State laws. Note the Tort Reform Law that passed unanimously just this fall with input from a mere 2,000 physicians from the State of Pennsylvania. I would caution those that would say the change is inherently bad or

wonderful. As we sit here this evening, not just men and women or PCP's and specialists, but clinicians and others focused on the health care of this community. We are representatives of 828 members of this melting pot of dedicated individuals that is Forbes Medical Staff. As part of this change, I am looking forward to working with you. I am honored to be working for you as the President of your Medical Staff for this next year. I look forward to your input. I will appreciate your assistance and together we can meet the changes that lay ahead. Thank you. Let's have a good year!

Being in the right place at the right time can give us opportunities to make a difference.

Tom welcomes LT to Promises Kept Farm

CHAPTER THIRTY-NINE
It's A Boy!

It was lunchtime during Spring Gobbler hunting season, when we got an unexpected telephone call that changed our family forever. Tom and his Dad had just come in from hunting on our farm and I was fixing lunch. The telephone rang. It was the adoption agency. "If you want a boy, we will be there in the morning."

When I could get my jaw off the counter, I gasped, "Okay!"

He was just two weeks old. They were coming from Washington. Tom asked, "Which Washington?"

"Sweetheart, I did not ask how many limbs the child had; I did not ask which Washington."

We had no infant supplies in the house. Tom and his Dad went to a local drug store to shop. Between them, they hunted down every item on the premises that said "child" or "baby." Tom's Dad got the jumbo jar of petroleum jelly for diaper rash. Tom purchased the individually-wrapped applicators of diaper rash cream. When they were done with their hunting that day, we were well supplied for months to come.

Ten of us met the beautiful boy that next day in our living room at Promises Kept Farm. He was chubby and happy, with a mop of dark hair and beautiful long eyelashes. There was a whirlwind of paperwork, forms to be filled out, a home inspection to accomplish, an attorney to meet to finalize the adoption. None of us thought to ask if he had been from D.C. or the State of Washington.

I had named Sikira, with the promise that Tom could name the next child. Maybe I did not think there ever would be a next child, but suddenly, here he was. Tom and I had each been named after our fathers. I was the second L.H. Fuge; he was the second Tom. My Dad's first name is Lloyd. Tom came up with the idea to name him after *both* Grandfathers. His name would be "Lloydthomas," all one word, eleven letters. His middle name would be Joseph after Tom's Grandfather. I told Tom that the poor kid would never finish writing a school paper; it would take so long just to write his name. But per our promise and with his sister's consent, Lloydthomas Joseph, he became. We called him LT for short. Sikira called him "ET."

Hundreds of photos later, our new addition had been passed around the room several times to be held by all. LT was no longer seeing any humor in it and proceeded to cry, loudly. Sikira, always sensitive to noises, asked us to "turn him off." We explained that her baby brother did not come with an on/off switch. "Then take out his batteries!" she suggested.

LHF teaches Resident Physicians with humorous stories

CHAPTER FORTY
It Could Be Raining

I have always been frustrated when I don't get a straight answer about things and in medicine, it has been no different.

In 1988, when I was adding administrative duties of Associate Medical Director to chairman, teacher and office Family Practitioner, my life seemed like a jigsaw puzzle. The Medical Director then had been a Radiologist before retiring from patient care. Though often an ally, I teased him about those in his field of medicine's lack of willingness to give an exact answer. I explained the vacillations of Radiologists to the young doctors with this story.

You could be standing by the window with a Radiologist looking through the pane, discussing the weather. Watching the drops fall, he would turn to you and say, "It could be raining. Cannot rule out someone on the roof urinating, consider aerial view." On a particularly bad day, he would say, "Consider satellite view," and end with, "Well, you could go outside and look." The parallel medical terms in their reports would be "Considered a CT scan or an MRI." "Clinically correlate" or "Figure it out for yourself" stood for "please go outside and look."

I half expect to hear my irreverent portrayal of radiology on some TV spoof. I have explained it with a wink to resident doctors for many years. I wonder if, whenever they get an unresponsive comment back, if my former students smile and think, "Well, it could be raining."

For years I have welcomed young doctors to our local community hospital to begin their extensive training in Family Practice. To uplift and entertain, for a greeting, I often recall a speech at MIT, which said, "If they had a good place to stand, they could build a lever and move the world." I assure those fortunate enough to be joining our ranks that this is "a good place to stand." From Family Practice, a young doctor could go anywhere.

I've congratulated more than one hundred on their completion of three years' training. Graduations were a time for me to recall my father, the other L.H. Fuge. At my wedding, he recalled Omar Khayyam's translation of a portion of the Rubaiyat:

The Moving Finger writes; and, having writ,
Moves on: all your Piety nor Wit
Can lure it back to cancel half a Line,
Nor all your Tears wash out a Word of it.

He went on to say:

We are writing new paragraphs in our lives,
We've been blessed.
And while our multi-syllabic cerebrations
may not make much sense nor be remembered long,
we ended with a prayer that these last few words would
be recalled:
Via Con Dios, "Go With God."

I have tried each year to share a part of myself. My goal

each time was to move listeners to think, if not to cry. For graduation of the senior Residents of Forbes Family Practice, I was asked to share comments in June of 2006. Because I had laryngitis, I took my two children with me. LT was only seven. He stood on a chair at the podium and read a short piece. "Mom wasn't sure if she would have a voice, and so she brought help." He paused. I waved. They laughed and clapped. After finishing the few sentences that I had written, he stepped down and walked his sister to the microphone.

I am told that Sikira has perfect pitch. I cannot even sing in the shower, so I can only say that she sounds like an angel to me. Music folks are impressed to hear that she can hit a high C. I am impressed that she can sing equally well with out music to accompany her. She proved it that day for the graduation when she sang "Climb Every Mountain," flawlessly. Though I have done dozens of speeches, many have told me that this—the one when I did not utter a sound—was my best ever.

LHF and children at Forbes Family Practice Residents' graduation

LHF tries to take Sikira for a ride on her new tandem bike

CHAPTER FORTY-ONE
Birthday Mix-up

When we go somewhere, everybody else in the family is dressed and in the car, ready to go sooner than I am. Of course, part of my job as family coordinator, is to help and motivate everyone else.

There's my daughter. Sikira wanted to wear something pretty for her birthday. She'd gone through her drawers, cupboard, and armoire, discarding previously favorite items. At thirteen, she was a newly, typical fashion-conscious teenager. Too short, too simple. Wrong color, wrong material. Using her fingers as guides, pulling out one, then another, she ransacked through them until Mom arrived.

I am a pack rat, daughter of a collector, tightly constrained by our little farm house's lack of storage. If I see something that would be perfect for someone I love, in the future, I get it and put it away. There are two important caveats to this particular method of shopping: one, either have an unlimited supply of cash, or purchase items at a good sale price; and two: be able to find your stored treasurer later when you need it. Let me just say for the record the second does not always work out for me. For this birthday, I found the perfect long-sleeved shirt decorated with roses. Sikira was thrilled.

Sikira had already started working on her beautiful, long mane of hair by the time I arrived. She had learned to tie back her tresses with decorative elastic bands, despite the trouble she'd had with dexterity since childhood. Today, the rest of her hair left something to be desired. Braided bangs would keep stray strands out of her eyes. Hair accomplished!

Nothing to do but put on jeans. What else would offset such a perfect outfit for a thirteen-year-old's birthday? You might not think it would be so difficult to choose such a simple item as blue jeans. Sikira finally selected. Tom can't imagine how our child ends up with so many clothes in her hamper. After "helping" her dress, it is no longer a mystery to me.

We were going for an early lunch to get seats for eight, as Sikira's restaurant of choice does not take reservations. It was time to step up the pace; unfortunately, my son was nowhere to be found. Although I had kissed LT and sung good morning on my way into our teenage daughter's room, he had not materialized from under the covers of his bed. Heading in his direction, I was ambushed by our four-legged family members.

We have raised Akita dogs for the last fifteen years. We built a set of kennels that guard the entrance road between the home and the stables. Luxury design now, they had gone from gravel to concrete with drains. With six foot fences and sunscreen-canopied runs, the dogs prefer to get out and run in these areas. Running on concrete keeps their toenails trimmed.

My husband has added the occasional hunting dog to our collection. They have thin coats and bodies. They eat enormous amounts of food in comparison to their weight. I have come to affectionately call them the "mouths with feet," in part because of their voracious appetite, but in part because of their incessant noisemaking. Howling, yapping, barking, crooning, they are continuously mobile: jumping, bouncing, pawing, moving. My husband calls the current example, his "dog on crack." Tom warns our children of the perils of drug use: "You could end up seriously skinny, bouncing off the walls, in constant trouble for your mouth, and spending much of your time in the doghouse."

With the first threat of snow, the kennels are closed for the winter. My pleadings, along with those of the children bring the dogs indoors for inclement weather. With the dirt and smell, dander and loose hair proliferated in their outdoor surroundings, it is quite an event to clean up our four legged family members to move inside. An assembly line starts with Tom in the shower ferrying one "four-legger" after another. Tom has the least sensitive of the skin and the strongest arms to wrestle critters unhappy with the concept of getting shampooed. Akitas can weigh more than a hundred pounds. Tom's special shower has a seat built in to accommodate his leg difficulties. It has ample room, but dogs explode out of it, like popcorn. My job, and the children's, is to corral the critters with large, fluffy towels and dry them off before they shake, or roll throughout the house.

We had just gone through this process, the night before Sikira's birthday. Excited after being inside and having licked up who-knows-how-much shampoo, the dogs' bowels and bladders were insisting on attention. With the parade of the four-leggers taken care of, it was back to my son, still in bed.

When we were growing up, for special events, maybe Sundays, my family could request special foods. Homemade pancakes, especially for my father. Sikira loves pancake or toaster made French toast. Our kids had finally outgrown their milk and egg allergies. My daughter especially enjoyed having a little cup of dipping syrup. The offer of this treat, or perhaps the threat of missing out, finally mobilized my son. He got as far as the bathroom. While he's cornered on the commode, I strip off his night clothes. Next I lay out, down to the underwear and belt, exactly what he should wear to "look nice" for his sister's birthday. We have less than two hours.

Before leaving for the birthday meal, we wanted to show Sikira her beautiful, new, blue two-wheel bike. Without vision, you might imagine that it would be tough for our daughter to ride a two-wheeler. At her Slippery Rock College Adaptive Sports Program in the summer, we had learned about something called tandem biking. This was the old "bicycle built for two" concept. The person with no vision rides in the second seat. The person with vision steers. They both peddle. Sikira found it delightful. I looked into acquiring such an apparatus. The price, a ridiculous sixteen hundred dollars. A local store could order one in the spring for a mere twelve hundred. They had sold many to the local School for the Blind in Pittsburgh over the years. A less sturdy model was six hundred dollars.

God bless the internet. On eBay, I found one for one hundred and thirty-five dollars. My husband was convinced that this "bargain" would come in a box without directions and not enough pieces, or be made of plaster of Paris or some other useless material, if it arrived at all. I sent my money on September 17. As of October 12, we had not seen it. I thought that perhaps Tom would be right, as he often is. Finally, a delivery truck arrived in the middle of the night, with a long, flat box. The birthday surprise arrived unassembled, without enough pieces, as Tom had predicted. Tom finalizing the assembly without directions, adapting pieces to fill in the holes that didn't come with nuts, bolts, or screws that would hold the handle bar and seats in place.

In our spare minutes before we left for lunch, this birthday gift was unveiled. Sikira was enthralled. LT miraculously appeared, dressed to participate. The idea was that I would drive Sikira around on the bike. Dad assured me it would take three people to help me onto the bike. Undeterred by his skepticism, we managed to get both my daughter and myself on the apparatus. My husband steadied us and managed to jump to the side to take her picture before I shakily took off down the road, squealing the whole way about my distress at the tiny little seat pinching into unmentionable places. My legs were weaker than they needed to be to propel the enormous metal frame. My balance was significantly shakier than it had been thirty years ago, the last time I had ridden a two-wheeler. We had not traveled far before I knocked the entire bike over—and us with it. Sikira landed on her feet. I did not. My husband, Tom, bravely offered to try. With help, Tom managed to lift his leg over the bike to get onto the seat. He managed to ferry our daughter half the length of our quarter-mile driveway, with me snapping pictures behind them all the way, and our son, on his little two-wheeler on training wheels, pedaling furiously behind them.

We found out the reason for the low price when my husband tried to turn the bike. A strong man despite his disabilities, Tom pulled sharply on the handlebars to start the bike turning back in our direction. The handlebars bent perpendicular to the tire without moving the bike at all. That was the end of the father and daughter bike ride.

Not wanting his sister's day to be ruined, LT offered to let her ride his bike. "Don't worry, Sis. I'll help ya." Always game for something athletic, my tall daughter proceeded to fold herself onto her brother's tiny blue bike. Her knees splayed to the sides like a clown's in a circus ride. Our son gave her a push. "It doesn't fall over," he reassured her. Some of the best pictures of the day were our son, walking alongside his sister. Sikira furiously pedaling the tiny little bike, LT giving verbal directions and encouragement.

My husband got dressed by stepping into a pair of jeans and a clean shirt. Tom was "ready" to go. I, on the other hand, was not.

Presents to be collected. Coupons and a wallet to be found. Extra cash to be scrounged to take with us for a tip.

Time for coats. Assist the children. My pockets stuffed. Kleenex. A spare pair of gloves, kids' toys. I was the last person to get into the car. As usual.

A mile down the road, I remembered we had no blank cassette tape with us. Sikira had wanted to tape record her event. Hurrying to the restaurant, I tried to explain to my husband as he drove, using our own version of sign language, since our daughter has excellent hearing. "We need to swing by the store to pick up what I forgot."

Tom did not comment on how many times I can forget things. We continued on. I figured he would just pull in to the closest store to the restaurant. I could run in and acquire a tape or two. Tom drove straight past the store. I guessed he planned to make a return trip. I made a sign in the air for a small rectangle object, explaining, silently, what it was we needed. Tom motioned back, "What kind?"

Well, frankly, I didn't care what company made the darn tape. I said, "I don't know."

He dropped me off at the curb by the restaurant. His parents have already arrived. "How many?" he asked before he drove away.

"One, two, whatever." Off he goes with our spare cash, back down the road to the store.

When Tom returned, there beside him on the seat were two beautiful long-stem orange roses. "Where was the tape?"

"What tape?"

"The tape to tape the party. That's what you went for."

"I went for roses. What are you talking about?"

Our communication was a little off. Tom went back for blank tapes. Sikira loved the flowers and the tape. Unfortunately, the batteries we brought for the tape player were defunct. The communication fiasco of the day produced two beautiful orange roses, but Sikira had to wait for more batteries to record her thoughts about her birthday. Me, I got the spare tapes for recording more family memories for this book.

Archibold M. Duff, Civil War veteran and wife

CHAPTER FORTY-TWO
Communication

As a young physician in Family Medicine, I took care of patients of all ages. Being close to patients was important, but I found out the hard way that they tended to share their "bugs," not just their stories. Youngsters seemed especially good at sharing the three "S's": slobbers, snots, and s… (One mother called them "stinkies".) I myself was therefore, often ill. Later in my career, I came up with the rule: "No Hugs for Bugs!" and got ill less frequently.

Laryngitis was the worst, trying to talk and give advice when I wanted a fire extinguisher for the pain in my throat. One fateful day, when I had been up taking phone calls through the night, I had no voice left at all by the time I had to go in to the office. Writing notes furiously to the office staff, I informed them that I actually felt better, but that we should offer to reschedule patients, as I could not utter a sound—let alone verbal advice. Dutifully the ladies called the twenty-two people who were scheduled to come in that day. Not one of them wanted to cancel. They all wanted to come meet with the doctor who could just listen! All day I listened, jotting brief notes in response to each patient. They all seemed satisfied. I learned that if I just listen, people can share with me what I need to know to help them.

Communication is funny like that; people need to feel there is a connection. It does not even have to be spoken. My Father told me a story about our family during the Civil War. Communication was difficult then. It was hard to hear from or about the safety of loved ones fighting in the conflict. A common belief was if you set a Mason jar upside-down on a fence post and it stayed safe, he would come home safe. If it fell, he had died.

Dad's great grandfather, Archibald M. Duff, was in the fighting at Gettysburg. He was gravely wounded and left for dead on the battlefield for days. At home, the Mason jar the family watched each day cracked, but did not fall. The family was relieved, but not surprised when he was finally ferried home alive by Roman Catholic nuns. Maggots had infested his leg wound and eaten away the gangrene until he was found and tended. Though devout Protestants, the family felt that their prayers had been answered by God sending the nuns to find and rescue Pap. His safety had been communicated through superstition.

Later in life, Pap protected his family by shooting two robbers at his home. One of the intruders was fatally wounded. Though finally acquitted of all charges, Pap had to endure years of court proceedings before his name was cleared. Pap himself was shot coming back into the house one night from the outhouse. Near deaf, he did not hear his son-in-law's charge to "stop and identify yourself." Pap refused to be taken to the hospital for treatment until the local constable came and took down his statement that this had "only been an accident" and "the boy was not to blame!" His insistence on this crucial communication saved the family any risk of the court troubles he had had, but cost him his life.

Tom teaches LT archery*

CHAPTER FORTY-THREE
Huntress

I am proud of being a hunter, most of the time. Not when I waste time and money *hunting* for my latest piece of china or crystal, but most of the time. Shopping is not my primary vice, but I have been known to spend too much at times. Surely, credit cards and eBay must be works of the Devil, or I must be the weakest sinner for as easily as I can let myself be pulled into debt. No crowds or traffic to fight through, no waiting for the "paper money" as we tell our children, to be earned. This kind of shopping is painless until the bill arrives—with interest charges. My Kid sister warns me about eBay's dangerous pull, which is only fair since she introduced me to it. Tom and I have made a spending limit; we do not go past that amount without consulting each other first. I am not a neurosurgeon or even a surgeon's wife so *moderation* and common sense have to prevail.

Our little farmhouse holds an odd combination of the crystal I have collected, along with stuffed animals. I am a teddy bear fan myself, but years ago my friend and nurse, "Miss Mary" started Sikira on a collection of different stuffed animals with unique shapes and textures by giving her a little stuffed anteater. Our stuffed animal collection, however, goes beyond the children's Beanie Baby collection, to include taxidermy.

Imagine the school's field trip to the museum, all those eager faces lighting up at the displays of stuffed wildlife, preserved and displayed for their education and amusement. Picture the youngster in the back seat of the car, face pressed to the pane, scanning the passing fields and forests for sheep or cow, bear or deer. Watch the family nature show, looking and learning about distant lands and native creatures. Now try to picture them with your eyes shut. What wouldn't I give to let my daughter "see" those animals?

We raise pigs and kittens, puppies and ducks. We teach them to be gentle so our children can handle them. Sikira has handled a baby horse, and nestled ducklings to her cheeks, but when she asks can she please see the groundhog, squirrel, fox or bear, we were at a loss.

Tom likes to hunt. Since having a family, he has done more planning and dreaming than actual hunting. He researched trips out to the western United States for elk, buffalo or antelope. For a week, even with other hunters and a shared guide, it could cost thousands for a chance at *one* animal. Looking at hunting shows and magazines, he had wistfully asked me about going to Africa. "When Hell freezes over," was my immediate reply.

When I met professional hunters from Combretum Safari in South Africa at a dinner for a Pennsylvania Conservation Group, they made us an offer worth considering. A whole African package for less than one week in the USA. The two weeks in South Africa would be in June, July or August – their winter. Tom inquired, "who are you and what have you done with my wife?'

It would be eighty degrees during the day, but no rain, no bugs and no shots! The package included all our meals, room and board, one on one with the Professional Hunter, side trips for photographs, daily laundry service, porters, and *five* plains animals to harvest. If you didn't get all your trophies, the price would be *prorated down*!

I would not go without my children. When we were growing up Kid and I vacationed with our folks. Mom said that when we flew, she was comforted to know that if the plane went down, we would all be together. To this day, I am not so fond of flying. My six-year-old told me not to worry. "We can put the back seat back into the Jeep, Mom, and drive you to Africa."

Traveling with children can be such a joy, if you let it. They see wonder in everything. After the hostess' safety talk on the plane, the kids talked endlessly about wanting to crash on the water versus the land. They wanted to try out the floatation devices and the slides to exit the plane.

I decided that I would hunt, but just for one animal that "better be bigger than my husband's." My request was answered when I dropped a Greater Kudu from one hundred and ten yards with just one shot to the heart. It was the best native food we had during our trip. Nothing is wasted of an animal there. The locals are *thrilled* when a visitor harvests an animal. Meat is not exported; they can have enough from one successful hunt to feed the whole village and have bones to make wares to sell. The hunter may have the hide, skull, horns and memories to take home.

I was not always such an assured hunter. When we moved to our farm, I started out by getting rid of groundhogs. Their holes were a hazard for our livestock. If a horse damaged a leg stepping into one, it might need to be put down. Tom teased that I waited to shoot until the animals were close enough to hit with a frying pan. Still, one shot is all I needed to quickly and humanely dispatch the unwanted intruders.

After our vehicle was totaled, I was bored with the repetitive physical therapy. Tom had a bow custom built for me. I practiced with him in a local league until my arm was strengthened and rehabilitated; I was able to archery hunt deer on our property. Deer was good eating and cheaper than the meat at Giant Eagle.

Our son is learning to appreciate archery, and we teach him to revere nature as a special gift from God. We appreciate the animals that assist, feed or clothe us. Who has not had a rabbit's foot or a leather jacket, a suede purse or shoes?

You might wonder how I could possibly get joy out of a stuffed animal hanging in my house. My daughter gets to touch or hold that real part of nature. Tom was asked by LT's elementary school, and took the whole collection there for "Art Appreciation Day." My blind Mother, this year for Thanksgiving, got to "see" a wild turkey in full strut. She says she had never understood or believed the plush replicas she had touched for decades.

Thanksgiving is an awesome time! Tom and I have hosted the family that day for many years. We plan special foods, cook for days, and give thanks for the many Blessings we have shared. We each talk about what we are grateful for at Thanksgiving. Sikira is grateful for time to visit with Family. Me, I think I am grateful that I am a hunter.

I hunt for food, but I have also hunted for companionship, friendship, and love. I have hunted for autonomy, authority, forgiveness and respect. I have hunted for medical solutions for decades. I try always to *hunt* for an honest, kind thing to say. I *hunt* for knowledge and acceptance and peace. I *hunt* for the beauty in each moment. When one of my crystal mugs got cracked and broken this Thanksgiving, I paused and was grateful that my Dad had gotten to enjoy a drink of milk in it, that it wasn't packed away in a box somewhere, unused. Most of the time, I am proud and grateful that I am a hunter.

LHF runs EKG on Dad

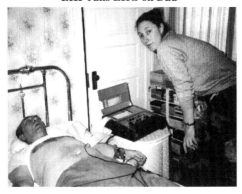

CHAPTER FORTY-FOUR
Faith

Over the years that I have spent learning and practicing medicine, one of the most important things I have found is that the patients have faith in their physician. I have been blessed to build thousands of relationships between myself and my patients, based on a sacred trust that I would do everything I could for them. I would work to find them their answers or find them somewhere or someone who could help, if need be. I would never lie to them. Regardless of what they would have to go through, I would be there with them; they would not be alone. It is not so much that the patients chose to walk with me, as that they chose to let me walk with them. I have felt honored by the faith that they have placed in me.

There is an old saying that pertains to medicine, that, "if you choose to care for yourself, you have a fool for a patient." It is difficult to be objective with yourself, perhaps even more difficult to be objective with your parents.

It can also be tough to have faith in the person whose diapers you changed, whose homework you helped with, and whose misbehaviors you corrected. Perhaps that is why the AMA, the American Medical Association, frowns on caring for one's own parents as patients. This year, I found myself stepping on that line and testing faith.

It started with this summer's family vacation. The folks have been fortunate to be able to take the family for extended vacations on different summers. My patient care responsibilities have not afforded me time off to join them on these excursions. My sister still talks about riding horseback on the beach.

This summer, it was some snazzy resort in Cancun, Mexico. Again, I would not be free to go. My family and I stayed home, only to get a phone call. My sister, distress in her voice, informed me that Dad had taken ill. Some stomach thing, she called it, with vomiting and diarrhea. It had gone on and on for days. He was not able to take food or water. This may have started with some water somewhere away from the resort.

Dad had not been able to take his usual medications. He was quite ill. The scenario went on and on. We were able finally to arrange transportation back home—not to our Pittsburgh Airport, but to New Jersey. We felt that if things were bad enough there, he could be hospitalized in the USA.

Miraculously, despite mom and others starting to take ill, we were able to get them all onto a small plane in New Jersey to the Pittsburgh Airport. I met them on the runway. Though airport security was tight, with my office T-shirt with embroidered logo, plus my name on a little cardboard medical ID with no photo, I was able to pass through one security level after another. I brought my doctor's bag with a stethoscope and a jug of paregoric, a liquid that does not require an injection to slow profuse diarrhea and vomiting. I acquired a wheelchair and the help of airport staff with an additional wheelchair to stand at the airplane door to ferry my disembarking family.

My sister recalls that when she saw me and threw her arms around my neck, a huge weight was lifted from her shoulders. She had faith that things would be okay. I do not know that my folks had any such faith. We put them into wheelchairs and pushed them to the vehicle I had waiting, parked literally right at the opening of the airport door. I had set up piles of blankets on the seat, with plastic in case of diarrhea. I had brought changes of clothes and small garbage cans for throwing up. I drove my parents to the local hospital that they requested. They were seen in the Emergency Room, tested and admitted—chest x-rays, EKG's. Before this trip, they had both been the picture of health: feisty, intelligent, demanding—almost arrogant.

Dad never really seemed quite himself after Mexico, plagued with night-time fever, sweats and weight loss. I was shocked to learn that between June and August he had lost thirty pounds. Dad seemed very tired and spent most of his time resting in bed. I was shocked to see my Dad in a T-shirt, because I could see the bones of his shoulders and ribs outlined. I gasped, "Get a chest x-ray *now*," thinking what I often have for patients—that there will be bad news. It could be cancer and in someone who had used tobacco in the past, this was a likelihood.

On my mother's birthday this year, I called the folks to explain the x-ray report. There was a ten centimeter mass in my father's chest.

I called the specialist. This could be a T4, N2, Stage IV Cancer. The numbers and letters rolled off her tongue like some foreign language I had not studied for the last decades of my life. All I kept hearing in my mind was, "This is bad. This is really bad."

Then, she said the two words that would stay with me, "six months." Then, "Six months if we treat it quickly and aggressively." There would be chemos, at least two, and radiation.

I thought to myself, "And Prayer."

My sister and I went to our folks' home with our husbands and children. We talked for hours. This was past concerning; this was dire. Dad would qualify for hospice. What did he want to do? How did he want to spend what days there would be? I remember Mom asking if we believed in God, her tone sad and sharp, as if to say she could not if this could happen to the one she loved. I tried to find the words, as I had for so many families before ours, that "there must have been a little angel sitting on his shoulder that we were able to find this now." or "Not everyone has the chance to say what they want to say." Some folks are lost abruptly, with no chance to prepare themselves or their families. Others suffer for extended periods, unable to speak or walk. Those fates, it seemed, Dad would be spared. I remember my sister saying that she believed in prayer and my mother crying.

My dad reflected that he had read just recently that "over one hundred billion Homo Sapiens had died on this planet over the years," and that he would be no exception.

It was a tough day. As we drove home, my father called my cell phone. I have often ended our calls with, "I love you," and never had a response in kind. It seemed an appropriate closing at the end of our call. "Pleasant dreams. I love you, Dad."

He responded, "I love you all, too." I cannot recall him having said it before.

I guess we each have faith in each other and the Lord in our own way. Dad has always chosen to express his love in actions and never in words. On the day we had to talk about goodbye, he reached out. Dad's expression of love seemed to show faith in his family, faith in me.

I have been blessed all my adult life to have met many good and devout people. I know, as I sit here near dawn and watch the glimmer of sunrise penetrate the night and the mists of the morning softly rise outside my window that others pray even now for my family. My father may leave us soon. Likely, it is cancer. I do not know that I can say I feel comforted, but I am peaceful.

I have had to tell hundreds of patients and their families over the years about cancer diagnoses. I would be sick to my stomach and my head would hurt. Often, I would feel tears inside me. I would hold their hands, look into their eyes, put my arm around their shoulders or hold their heads against my chest. I would tell them. I would be there for them. Whatever lay ahead, we could do it together. I have no such internal anguish this week when I think about my father. Perhaps that is the comforting Spirit of our Lord that enlightens me.

I have often said that we are more fortunate than most. We have been given a wonderful gift – time to say the things that we have not said, to forgive what we have not forgiven, and the knowledge that we must take the time *now* to enjoy each other's company because time is short.

The biopsies and samples of the nodule in the lymph nodes and mass in my father's chest have been sent to the lab. In hours or days we will have the answers about what is ravaging his lungs and sapping his strength. We will know the name to put to the disease that is taking him from us now. I might have said that there is nothing to do but pray and wait, but I have come to know that it is time to enjoy, appreciate and give thanks for this special gift of knowledge in this small window of time. I find myself giving thanks at this odd hour and saying a short prayer that has come to be mine in the last ten or twenty years: "guide our feet on the path You would have us walk. Amen."

I am writing this now because I want to capture that feeling I had that I want to do all I can for him. I will find out what he needs, I will take care of what he needs or find someone who will. He will not have to go through it on his own.

Since then, we have had more than a year of days together. The mass has shrunk to one centimeter. Dad is off most medicines. I do not call it a miracle. I do not dare to hope. Some days are good, some are bad. I figure every day each of us gets is a gift.

God protects us all as we travel this Life, like this African walkway gives beauty and safety against crocodiles. We just have to look at things in the right light and with the right perspective.

Photo by LHF - 2005 in South Africa

ABOUT THE AUTHOR

LaDonna H. Fuge is a lifetime resident of Pennsylvania. Dr. Fuge graduated from Gannon University in Erie PA before earning her MD from Hahnemann Medical School in Philadelphia, now called Drexel University. She is board certified and a Fellow of the American Academy of Family Practice. L H Fuge MD has spent twenty years splitting her time and talents between patient care, teaching, administrative medical work and her family.

Dr. Fuge and her "CARE Team" start each office meeting with a smile. The CARE Team has assisted her in sharing a positive approach to patient care. Believing that: "if no one takes the time to educate the next generation, what will happen to *all* of us?" Dr. Fuge has mentored medical students in her office, from a number of medical schools, including Pitt, Temple and Hahnemann. She has been privileged to work with and teach young Family Physicians in the hospital, from the Forbes Residency each year since 1992.

First born child of local parents with strong civic and philanthropic interests, Dr. Fuge had an eclectic upbringing that included Bible School at the Untied Presbyterian Church and dancing on pool tables in short skirt and cowboy hat for her father's "FUGE Team" political rallies. Before her expeditious if circuitous journey to become a physician, she enjoyed chairing the Philanthropies Committee of the Clairton Women's Club with her mother. Now Dr. Fuge is donating the monies from this publishing of her book to Forbes Hospital Foundation.

Dr. Fuge lives with her family on their small Pennsylvania farm. Her children have seen her personally run for and be elected to various medical staff officer positions from chairman to treasurer to president. Dr. Fuge teaches by example that "we need to speak up when we can, especially for those that cannot." LaDonna strives to show her children that they too can *do* many things in their lives; appreciate *each* day and aspire to *be* happy.